BOWS OF BURNING GOLD

Helen Carey

'Bring me my bow of burning gold!
Bring me my arrows of desire!'
William Blake

Published by *Alfresco Books* in September 2005
Reprinted in November 2005
Mill Race, Kirkby Malham, Skipton, BD23 4BN
Telephone: 01729 830868
E-mail: jen@alfrescobooks.co.uk

A CIP record for this book is available from the British Library.

ISBN: 1 873727 22 4

Publisher's Note: While every effort has been made to ensure that the information given in this book is correct the publisher does not accept responsibility for any inaccuracy.

Cover
Rob Jones, Graphic Design, Cheshire County Council

Design and Typesetting
Jen Darling of *Alfresco Books*

Printer
Ashford Colour Press, Gosport

Special thanks to *LoSalt* for sponsoring this book.

FOREWORD

I first met Helen Carey when she was an outstanding chairman of the Cheshire Federation of Women's Institutes. She was elected chairman of the National Federation in 1999 and served us all very well for four years. Her own special interest was to raise the profile of WIs on Public Question matters and on environmental issues in particular.

In my opinion, *Bows of Burning Gold* is a special and very entertaining book which any reader, whether a WI member or not, will greatly relish. It celebrates 90 years of Women's Institutes, the first of which opened in 1915 in my local village, Llanfairpwllgwyngyllgogerchwyrndrobwll-Llantysilio-gogogoch — the village on the Isle of Anglesey with the longest name in Britain.

When I married and came to live here in 1948, I learnt that the concept of the WI movement in Wales was the brainchild of my father-in-law's cousin, Colonel Stapleton Cotton, who, on becoming paralysed, had come to live with his wife on the Anglesey estate in 1915. He was very involved in the rural and agricultural life of Anglesey, and in the part that women might play in it.

Helen Carey's structure for the book is brilliant. There is a page for every year and each includes a brief summary of the developing story of the WI, locally, nationally and internationally. Each 'year' page also includes Helen's choice of one or two world events and a resolution which has been discussed and voted upon in each WI, then following endorsement at the AGM, is acted upon locally and nationally. In 1972, for example, the resolution put forward by the Anglesey Federation urged, 'the government to make it mandatory rather than permissive, as at present, for all local authorities to provide a full free Family Planning service'.

This is social history at its best and is often very funny too, for instance, in 1933 a 'teller' reported the Welsh conference as 'a bit mad' and said that she, 'couldn't control the chairman', who was Mrs Alfred Watt! And in 1936, a WI market producer sent in a turkey egg, priced at 3d, with the accompanying note, 'If you think the egg is too high, drop it'!

People of all ages will find something that relates to their own lives in this book. In my case I remember very well speaking as a member of the

Lady Anglesey with her children

National Executive, from the platform of the Albert Hall, when I was very visibly pregnant with my last child and, a little later on, going to Denman College as its chairman to help choose our new Welsh-speaking officer, breast-feeding that baby in between interviews!

I know you'll very much enjoy this book, which brings life in the WI so vividly to mind.

Shirley Anglesey
National Chairman 1966-69

CONTENTS

INTRODUCTION

'If you don't know your past you can manipulate the present. But you do need chronological milestones to understand where you are today.'

Tristram Hunt (historian and author)

The WI turns 90 this year, not a bad milestone from which to look back at some of the other milestones along the way; an opportunity, too. to remind ourselves of the important role the WI has played in the social fabric of our local communities and of our country.

This is not the definitive history of the WI. It is simply ninety snapshots across our history, capturing but a handful of the actions, events and determination that have made the WI what it is today — an organisation with as much relevance and value to this century as to the last.

The first Women's Institutes, founded by Adelaide Hoodless, were formed in Canada in 1897 and similar organisations were started in Belgium and Ireland in the early 1900s, several years before the formation of the first WI in Llanfairpwll in 1915. In each country it was the conviction that rural women had an important role to play in their local communities that led to the creation of the first Women's Institutes. There was a strong belief that, in order to fulfil this role, women needed education and encouragement, and that these could be found in the welcoming and safe environment of the new WIs.

Our early members always sought to balance the strong purpose of the WI with social, cultural and sporting activities. It is this balance that gives the WI its unique quality and provides the membership with so many opportunities. As one member put it,

> 'The WI gives the warmth of friendship, the sharing of laughter, the opportunity of widening horizons, together with the strength and unity gained by being part of a group of women at local and national levels.'

We all have different needs and wants at different times. Sometimes it might be to join a gardening group or a choir, or perhaps take part in a craft class. Another time it might be to get involved in the community, perhaps by clearing a pond or picking up litter, or lobbying for a bus route, a cycle path or a mobile library. On another occasion we might feel moved to speak up for fair trade or against domestic violence. Then again we might simply wish to go to the theatre or take a walk with friends. For 90 years the WI has provided a valuable forum for satisfying these diverse needs.

The constitutional aim of the WI has always been 'to improve the quality of life of the community' and our history shows the difference that women, working together, can make. Our policy has always been democratically determined through the resolutions we debate and approve at our AGM. These give members a mandate to speak out — to both local and national government — on the social, economic and environmental issues that concern them.

Our reason and integrity can still make a difference. The challenges facing us today are as important to women now as those that faced our earlier members. There is climate change, HIV/AIDS, and world debt for instance. Closer to home there's childhood obesity, waste disposal and accessible transport. Nothing gets done if we leave it to others and we are valued for the efforts we make. Perhaps that's why we tend to attract more members when we are seen to be active and responsible citizens.

I hope that members will use this book as a promotional aid and that they will be encouraged to delve further into our history. With this perspective from the past I hope that both they, and future members, will be inspired to take up some of the challenges facing us and, with their *bows of burning gold*, will build *Jerusalem*.

Summer house at Graig, Llanfairpwll, meeting place of first WI in Wales.

PREFACE

Firm foundations are needed for an organisation to survive and grow. Our early pioneering members gave the WI a strong foundation on which it could build and develop, and it is because of these strong beginnings that the WI has been able to evolve and flourish over the past 90 years. Each new decade brings fresh challenges and this book demonstrates that the WI has had the strength and vision to rise to the challenges that have faced it.

One of the abiding strengths of the organisation has been the important work that WIs and individual members have done in their communities. At certain times during the past 90 years many projects have been initiated that have focused members' minds on community action. Recently, the *Community Challenge Project* has done just that and it has been heartening and truly amazing to see and read about the number and quality of the projects that have been undertaken over the past three years. The *Community Challenge Project* has shown that WIs can play as vital a role in today's communities as they did in the past. It has also demonstrated that a partnership with the right commercial sponsor can bring added value and greater success, and we are very grateful to *LoSalt* for sponsoring and supporting our community challenges during the past three years.

As long as members continue to play an active and vital role in their communities and contribute to the wider needs of those around them, the future of the WI will be assured.

Barbara Gill
National Chairman, 2005

1915 – 1924

1918 Pruning test

1920 Early trading depot

1921 ***Oxfordshire****'s travelling exhibition*

1923 Visiting Switzerland

'What must be done is to develop to the fullest extent the two great social forces, education and organisation, so as to secure for each individual the highest degree of advancement.'

Adelaide Hoodless

'We, the members of the Llanfair Women's Institute, pledge ourselves to do our utmost to make the Institutes the centre of good in our neighbourhood'

Llanfairpwll WI

'A friend said, "Come along with me". I said, "No I'm not". But she kept bothering me and my husband said, "For goodness sake go with her and stop her worrying". So I went with her and that was the best day's work I ever did.'

A member in 1919

Home of Erland Lee – founder, with Adelaide Hoodless, of the WI movement – in the village of Stoney Creek, Ontario.

In 1920 there were 99,418 members.

1915

The resolution, 'that we form a Women's Institute (WI), affiliated to the Agricultural Organisation Society,' was taken on 16th September in **Llanfairpwll** on Anglesey. Its first official meeting was on 25th September and the special subject for discussion was *The Food Supply of the Country.*

Members of that first WI

This sounds straightforward. Decision taken. WI formed. Onwards and upwards! But it hadn't been that simple. Much lobbying from a strong-minded Canadian, Mrs Alfred Watt, with strong support from Mr Nugent Harris, Secretary of the Agricultural Organisation Society (AOS), had been needed to turn apathy, especially from women, into interest. Their determination was rewarded and in July 1915 Mrs Watt had been appointed to the AOS staff for three months as an organiser of WIs.

Llanfairpwll was her first success, swiftly followed by **Cefn** and **Trefnant** (Denbighshire) in Wales, and **Singleton** (Sussex) and **Wallisdown** (Dorset) in England.

In December, the Women's Institute (sub-committee of the AOS) adopted model rules for WIs, based on those of the Canadian WIs, which safeguarded the democratic structure of the organisation and defined its non-sectarian and non-party-political character.

Although WIs were formed with the long-term vision of filling 'a permanent need in the rural life of the nation', and not because of the need for women to play a major part in the war effort, it seems likely that this need must have acted as a catalyst. These new WIs were to provide a forum in which women could find their true role in society.

1916

... a time when all events were dominated by the First World War.

• • •

By the Autumn, 24 WIs had been formed and Mrs Nugent Harris was appointed by the AOS to be honorary Women's Institute secretary. Government departments, including the Board of Trade and the Board of Agriculture, were noting the value of the WIs and asked them to support the national effort by linking together women doing war work in rural areas, especially the newly formed Women's Land Army.

Grace Hadow (later national vice-chairman) founded a WI in **Cirencester** (Gloucestershire) and became president. In 1917, however, it was decided that WIs should only be formed in villages, where the need was greatest, and WIs which had been formed in towns became *centres*, providing services to rural areas when the need arose.

During the year, Alice Williams (later first honorary secretary, honorary national treasurer and editor of *Home & Country*) founded and became first president of **Deudraeth** (Meirionethshire). In 1917 this was the first WI to own its own hall.

Criccieth WI (Caernarfonshire) opened a small market stall 'in response to the urgent need for increased food production and distribution'.

In a letter to Mrs Alfred Watt in February, Colonel Stapleton-Cotton (whose wife was the first president of **Llanfairpwll** WI) wrote,

'In the Institutes you have absolute unselfishness as your ideal. Every member joining must ask herself not, 'What am I going to get out of this if I join?' but, 'If I join how can I help to better the lot of the whole community?'

Cirencester WI*'s Jam Factory, in full swing in 1916.*

1917

Czar Nicholas abdicates.

British Government allows women to become taxi drivers.

• • •

On 16th October, in the Central Hall, Westminster, the National Federation was formed at the first AGM of the Women's Institute organisation. 60 delegates were present and Lady Denman became its first chairman.

The Constitution and Rules were adopted and the Central Committee of Management was elected. Financial sponsorship for forming new WIs moved from the AOS to the Women's Branch of the Board of Agriculture's Food Production department.

From the outset, Lady Denman was determined that the organisation should be self-governing and the government of the day, appreciating the responsible and valuable role that members could play in their communities, assumed responsibility for the formation of WIs but left them alone to shape their own policy and rules.

With only three weeks' food supply left in the country, food production was a priority and at the AGM members were urged to, 'take every opportunity of becoming more skilled in land work and therefore in the production of food.'

The **Sussex** conference of Women's Institutes, at its formation meeting, recommended guidelines of work for increasing food production, developing village industries and preparing for reconstruction.

Queen Mary visited the Women's Institute National Economy exhibition in Hyde Park.

Toy making industries were set up and a 'topical toy rabbit, Cuthbert' made an appearance in **Sussex**. His topicality is not reported!

The year started with 40 WIs and finished with 140.

Resolution: *No Public Affairs resolutions this year. Resolutions concerning the Constitution and Rules were passed at the AGM.*

1918

Armistice signed on 11th November.

Representation of the People Act gives women over 30 the vote.

• • •

Lady Denman, writing in *The Landswoman* — the journal of the Land Army and the WI (volume 1) — said, 'More food is being grown. ... Women's Institutes can do an inestimable amount of good by keeping up the spirits of those in their village.'

Members were beginning to find their voice and, at the second AGM, a delegate from **Epping WI** (East Sussex) reported that, 'In rural areas the conditions are absolutely disgraceful. ... We must do all in our power to awaken people.'

Voluntary County Organisers (VCOs) were becoming increasingly active and the first residential VCO school was held at Burgess Hill, Sussex. It lasted three weeks!

Craft initiatives were taking place and, with encouragement from the National Executive who believed that old crafts could be re-established on a sound commercial basis, thus providing a livelihood for village women, trading groups were formed within some WIs. **Worcestershire**, however, expressed its disquiet at the 'introduction of all sorts of trading which was not in the spirit of Institutes'.

A founder member of **Truro WI** (Cornwall), writing in the 1970s, remembered its formation and 'a small room in a warehouse on Lemon Quay fitted out with reading and writing facilities, and open daily to members until 8 pm.' At one time this WI had a membership of over 600 and was reputedly the largest in the world.

Resolution: *Members urged ... to ensure that full advantage is taken ... of the government scheme for state-aided housing.*

***Epping WI**, Essex*

1919

Versailles Peace Conference.

Nancy Astor, first woman MP to take her seat in Parliament.

• • •

The vexed question of who governs the WI had been raised periodically and, at a Special General Meeting in October, the issue was finally decided. The National Executive committee would continue to be elected directly by the WIs and a new Consultative Council of County Federation representatives would be set up, to confer with and advise the Executive.

At the October AGM, the controversial resolution that, 'the National Federation of Women's Institutes (NFWI) be urged to consider the advisability of bringing men of the villages into the Institute movement', was lost.

Writing in the first issue of *Home & Country*, which appeared in March, Lady Denman wrote, 'Village will be united with village and county with county'. Mrs Alfred Watt described her visit to Sandringham to talk about the WI.

The NFWI appointed representatives to serve on the first Women's Committee of the League of Nations Union and an article in the *Farmer & Stockbreeder* stated that, 'The Women's Institute member is beginning to take a practical and active interest in public affairs'.

Stanwell WI (Middlesex) went to Hounslow barracks to buy an ex-army hut for its meetings and, when it finally became unusable, members campaigned, and were largely responsible for building their new village hall, which was opened in 2000.

Because of its trading activities, **Ninfield WI** (East Sussex) became affiliated to the Hastings branch of the National Union of Women Workers.

Lewes WI (East Sussex) opened a WI market and, by 1921, was selling produce from 23 nearby WIs.

No Public Affairs' resolutions this year.

1920

Council of League of Nations launched in London.

MPs pass Home Rule Bill for Ireland.

• • •

The NFWI became financially independent from the Board of Agriculture and the Development Commission gave £10,000 towards the general organisation and running of WIs. A Commission report commented on 'the extraordinary outburst of energy, resourcefulness and skill amongst rural women, evidence of which need only be sought in the activities of Women's Institutes'.

The Guild of Learners was formed, 'to improve conditions of rural life by encouraging home and local industries' and 'to regain the practice of home handicrafts with a view to restoring the best traditions of English workmanship'.

Concerned about funding for adult education, Grace Hadow, national vice-chairman, called a meeting of representatives from the YMCA, WI, Village Clubs' Association, and Workers' Educational Association, 'to consider co-operation in social and educational matters, and to prevent reduplication or checkmating one another's efforts'. From this meeting grew the first Rural Community Council (RCC).

Competitions for laundry were included in **Shropshire**'s first exhibition competitions. Professional laundresses could compete but not win prizes!

Oxfordshire discouraged bee-keeping because of a disease amongst bees on the Isle of Wight.

An **East Sussex** VCO reported, '...too much leaning towards amusements rather than educational subjects'.

Kings Langley WI (Hertfordshire) held a social evening with, 'Men invited. Husbands for choice!'

Resolution: *That it is advisable to have women's organisations, such as the Women's Institutes, represented on parish councils, district councils and sub-committees, to deal with health and housing.*

***Sandridge WI**, West Kent*

1921

Country's first birth control clinic opens in London.

Insulin is isolated, thus heralding a treatment for diabetes.

• • •

Although still receiving government grants, the NFWI was determined that the organisation would become financially self-sufficient and a 'permanent part of the rural life of the country'. A letter to the Treasury from the national treasurer reported, 'In addition to the payment of affiliation fees, almost every Institute has accepted the obligation of having at least one money-raising effort annually, the proceeds of which are to be divided between the County Federations (CFs) and the National Headquarters'.

The first federation secretary of **Lindsey**, Margaret Winteringham, was elected to parliament, becoming the first woman to represent a rural constituency. Her membership of the WI, she said, was the best training she could have had for her work as an MP.

The importance of training and education in its broadest sense was recognised and the first WI handbook appeared. The Consultative Council recommended that CFs should teach and instruct speakers on local government and that 'county representatives and educational experts' should discuss 'technical and higher education'.

The first County Music Festival was held in **East Sussex** with classes for WI choirs, mixed choirs and quartets.

Handicrafts were proving popular and, with 'an increasing desire for a higher standard of workmanship', area Handicraft Schools were in great demand.

The NFWI moved to 26 Eccleston Street.

Resolution: *That this meeting of the NFWI urges all women to support the principles of the Plumage Bill now before parliament.*

West Wittering WI*, West Sussex*

1922

First regular radio news broadcast.

Treasures of Tutankhamun unearthed.

• • •

The controversial question of men joining the WI has been raised from the organisation's earliest days. When the government's Development Commission was asked to help fund the work of the NFWI in 1919, it stipulated that the WI must have a working agreement with the Village Clubs' Association (VCA), a voluntary organisation set up, with encouragement from the government, to sponsor and encourage the building of village halls. Its aim eventually was to open membership to both men and women — a potentially rival group to the NFWI.

The VCA now proposed to form women's sections and the Development Commission suggested an amalgamation between the two organisations with a mixed Executive. A decision had to be made! The NFWI, realising that its independence would be lost forever, rejected the proposal. The organisation's self-determination was assured.

The Development Commission continued to support the NFWI but, when asked for funding to extend the NFWI's work to the Channel Islands and the Isle of Man, the Commission refused as its remit was confined to the UK.

14 WI students were instructed in 'sight-reading, conducting and melody-making' in an informal music school in **mid-Wales** and a **Worcestershire** member suggested that men should be included in WI choirs.

Bramham WI (Yorkshire) advocated a pooling of fares scheme at the AGM (finally passed in 1932).

Resolution *passed welcoming government action taken to combat venereal disease, and urging education on public health issues.*

NFWI Executive

1923

Bill passed allowing women to petition for divorce.

300,000 killed in Tokyo earthquake.

• • •

Interest in international affairs has always been encouraged and, with the personal advice and help of Sir Henry Lunn, the NFWI organised a ten-day visit to Switzerland for 50 members. 10 guineas covered the cost of all rail fares, hotel expenses and excursions!

A resolution on postal voting for the election of the NFWI executive members was passed and it was officially decided that membership was only open to women and girls.

Recognising the uniqueness and importance of the Welsh Federations, a Welsh speaking member was co-opted onto the NFWI executive and the first Welsh Counties' conference was held.

Cumbria opened its first permanent headquarters, in a prison cell, at an agreed cost of £5 per year.

Gloucestershire received an education grant of £250 from the County Council.

From the beginning, community involvement was stressed and WIs in **Surrey** helped clean up village ponds and collect empty tins and bottles.

Ringmer WI (East Sussex) bought a bath chair for the village which members could borrow for 1d a day or non-members for 3d. The chair was to be returned 'clean after use'.

It was suggested at **Solihull WI** (West Midlands) that if it joined the Solihull Poultry Society, at a cost of 5/- a year, members would be entitled to buy wire-netting, chicken food, and eggs for hatching, at a reduced cost.

Resolution *passed concerning the humane slaughter of animals.*

Partridge Green WI*, West Sussex*

1924

First telephone call between the UK and Australia.

Stalin emerges as strong man of Russia.

• • •

A training course for VCOs was held in Cambridge. Its main theme was agriculture and visits were made to farms run on Danish lines, and *Chivers'* fruit farm, to see jam making on a large scale!

Jerusalem was sung for the first time at the AGM, with an arrangement for string orchestra and women's voices specially composed for the WI by Sir Walford Davies.

There was an increasing interest in reading among members, who demanded greater access to books. Thanks mainly to lobbying from WI members, over 18 counties inaugurated rural library schemes. In many instances the WI acted as library agent for the village, receiving, distributing and changing books.

Education was a high priority and members urged County Councils to 'make full use of the opportunities for the development of adult education in rural areas, afforded by the WI movement'.

The Times declared that, 'The National Federation of WIs is one of those comparatively rare democratic bodies which do a large amount of useful work and say very little about it.'

Townswomen were not forgotten and, in July, **Overbury WI** (Worcestershire) entertained 62 women from the poorest quarter of Birmingham, paying for their lunch on the way down and providing a snack for the bus journey home.

Resolution: *That Women's Institutes be asked to use their influence to secure an increase in the number of women police throughout the country.*

***Ridlington WI**, Leicestershire & Rutland*

1925 – 1934

Craft Skills in the early years

Dressmaking class at ***Forton and Cleveley WI****, Lancashire*

Carpentry

A potter at work

Spinning

Knitting industry at ***Piddlehinton WI****, Dorset*

'In their WIs women have found something for themselves, a way of meeting across boundaries of class and denomination, a way of building a community of women able to explore their own skills and take charge of their own affairs without the controlling influence of men.'

Anne Stamper

Early women MPs — Margaret Winteringham and Lady Astor outside the Houses of Parliament.

In 1930 there were 291,570 members.

1925

***The Charleston* takes the UK by storm.**

First motel opens in the US.

• • •

10 years on from the birth of the organisation, its value and importance is clearly recognised.

A report of His Majesty's Inspectors, on the educational work of the Women's Institutes, concluded that,

> 'The ten years which have elapsed since the movement first became a national organisation shows results which can only be described as phenomenal. ... How long they will continue to be this vitalising power in the country remains to be seen but it is certain that village women must be among the leaders if it is to retain its distinctive character. That they are interesting themselves keenly in affairs of local and national import ... augers well for their future, while the brightness and interest the movement has brought into the lives of the women themselves is beyond all question'.

Recognising the problems facing the agricultural industry, the NFWI tried to rekindle a fresh interest in food production and the first school for agricultural speakers was held in Lichfield, Staffordshire, followed by another in Northampton. A Guild of Food Producers was suggested but the time wasn't right and members showed little interest.

Cambridgeshire bought and distributed over 12,000 bulbs.

Wall WI (Staffordshire) started a First Aid cupboard for the benefit of the village.

Brushford WI (Somerset) debated, 'Should the husband help in the home?'

***Resolution** concerning high level of maternal mortality associated with child-bearing and its effect on the health and welfare of families.*

***Epping & District WI**, Essex*

1926

John Logie Baird invents television.

A General Strike convulses the UK.

• • •

Life wasn't all 'high seriousness' in WIs and music, drama and dancing were always important activities.

One-day drama courses were held for drama producers and a combined music and drama conference led to a Drama Festival being held two years later in London.

Staffordshire awarded a shield to the WI with 'the best production of one scene from a Shakespeare play'. History doesn't relate which scene won!

The NFWI headquarters moved from 26 Eccleston Street to 39 Eccleston Street. Grace Hadow, national vice-chairman, welcomed the move as 'a change for the better'. It was a house where, 'The typists look over the tree-tops in the intervals of performing marvels with typing machines and with that mysterious object known as the Gestetner, which looks more like a chaff-cutter and turns out 50 copies a minute of any object entrusted to it.'

Over the years, comments have frequently been made about the amount of paperwork coming from national and federation offices. A **Worcester** member complained at the annual council meeting that, 'It is most undesirable that secretaries should learn to dread seeing envelopes sent from county'. And another grumbled that, 'Sometimes the amount of information forced down secretaries becomes almost indigestible'!

Resolution *concerning the Board of Education's report on the health of school children, with a suggestion that WI members may be of practical help in the matter of the health of children in rural areas.*

NFWI Executive

1927

First solo trans-Atlantic flight by Lindbergh.

Government says it will give women over 21 the vote.

• • •

The NFWI became independent from external funding, although funding was given for specific projects and events.

Under the chairmanship of Lady Denman, a government sub-committee continued to consider, 'the general question of the practical education of women for rural life'. Its findings, published in 1928 in the Denman Report, recognised the double contribution of village women to food production in both growing and cooking it. It concluded that all agricultural education should include household management.

Following this report, County Councils were encouraged to appoint suitably qualified women to their agricultural staff to train countrywomen in rural domestic economy. Until the outbreak of war in 1939 this was patchy.

Public recognition was given to **Worcestershire**'s Farm & Garden Guild (formed in 1923) when special classes for poultry and rabbits were granted to WI members by the Three Counties Society.

The *Southern Daily Echo*, on the occasion of the NFWI's 10th birthday, said that,

> 'The WIs have revolutionised rural life by awakening a spirit of corporate comradeship, practical endeavour and idealism. They definitely make life in country districts happier, more hopeful and more useful.'

Northamptonshire held its first tennis tournament.

Resolution: *The NFWI should consider the possibility of arranging for short courses in Domestic Science to include food values and household budgeting for WI members and should urge the county and other authorities to have special consideration for the needs of rural areas.*

NFWI Executive

1928

Alexander Fleming discovers penicillin.

Amelia Earhart flies the Atlantic.

• • •

'We live in an age when the public conscience is becoming more aware', members were told at the AGM. This sentiment illustrated the concerns during the year, which included rural water supplies, education of women for rural life, public telephones and women agricultural workers' wages.

At the Welsh Counties Conference WIs were urged, 'to endeavour to influence public opinion by every means in their power and to make greater use of facilities provided for teaching health and hygiene, with special reference to maternal mortality'.

The NFWI recommended **Staffordshire** not to start a WI in a barracks, 'although if it was open to anyone else living in the neighbourhood ... with equal opportunity for all to hold office' there would be no definite objection and they 'would be very interested to hear how the experiment worked out'.

The NFWI held its first Drama Festival and **Berkshire** performed a 'vigorous and spirited' historical pageant in Windsor Home Park. 200 members attended **East Sussex**'s annual conductors' course.

Supporting the RSPCA's campaign on animal slaughter, **Worcestershire** bought three humane killers to loan to them.

Shere WI (Surrey) resolved 'not to drop litter, to remove if possible any they see and to prevent others from spoiling the countryside'.

Resolution: *That this meeting ... desires to put on record its appreciation of the work done by the United Kingdom Carnegie Trust for country people and in particular of the great benefit conferred by the establishment of rural libraries.*

NFWI Executive

1929

First *green belt* area in the UK approved — near Hendon.

Black Thursday: Stock market crash on Wall Street in the US.

• • •

Improving the quality of life in the community has always been the fundamental aim and purpose of the WI from the time of its inception in Wales in 1915.

It is interesting, therefore, to read in an article, written nearly 15 years later by the National Union of Societies for Equal Citizenship, that 'there is no work today more necessary than the development of every woman into a conscious and effective citizen. ... All efforts to increase the health and well-being of the community depend for their success upon the intelligent co-operation of women in their homes'.

Items listed on the agenda for the List of Lecture Schools and Classes 1929-30 by Mrs Alfred Watt MA MBE include, 'The New Community Spirit' and 'Where there is No Vision the People Perish'.

For the first time a representative from the NFWI went to a conference of the International Council of Women held in Antwerp but, along with others from rural areas, came away disappointed. None of the issues facing rural people, such as clean water, education and transport had been discussed.

A National Handicraft Exhibition was held for one week in London and for a second week in Leeds. Queen Mary visited the exhibition and 'graciously accepted' a counterpane embroidered co-operatively by members from every federation.

Resolution: *This meeting urges every Women's Institute to study the work of the League of Nations and consider how best to further the cause of world peace.*

Berkshire

1930

Government rejects plans for a Channel Tunnel between England and France.

Frozen peas first put on sale in America.

• • •

A two-day AGM was held in Blackpool. Over 3,000 members travelled on a train 'a quarter of a mile long and labelled WI'. A BBC broadcast at 10.45 am included Lady Denman's address, a speech made by the president of the Board of Education and *Jerusalem.*

The national treasurer asked members to 'devote close attention to the money matters of their own WI and their Federation', as 'good service could only be given to members if the organisation was financially sound.'

A resolution, passed at a conference between the County Councils' Association and the NFWI, 'advised County Education Authorities to co-operate whenever possible with the NFWI in the provision of technical and adult education' and urged 'a broad view to be taken of the fundamental values of health, cooking, preserving, needlework, food production and marketing'.

Warwickshire held a Great Historical Pageant, with a cast of 5,000, to raise £5,000 'to place the federation on a sound financial basis'. The Birmingham City Orchestra provided the music and 20,000 spectators attended the event.

Home & Country recommended 'Science in the Home' (Pitman 2s 6d).

Little Clacton WI (Essex) raised money for funds by buying and hiring out a sweep's outfit. Members paid 6d and non-members 1s.

Resolution: *That this meeting is of the opinion that the punishment imposed in cases of cruelty to children is far from adequate.*

Brentwood WI*, Essex*

1931

Decision taken to introduce traffic lights throughout the country.

Chrysler Motor Company factory opens in England.

• • •

Facing a severe economic crisis, and appreciating that WI members had a special contribution to make, the government held discussions with the NFWI about setting up markets throughout the country. Greater emphasis was placed on training in cooking and nutrition.

500 **Bedfordshire** members took part in 'The Masque of Lady Margaret', the mother of Henry VII, who depicted someone who stood for the WI values of commitment, unselfishness, teamwork and friendship. The national press commented that,

> 'The spirit of the whole was marvellous for its unselfishness, kindliness and whole-hearted desire to achieve a worthy success. It has truly been a happiness for me to learn more of the WI movement in such a wonderful way'.

The need for local action in **Tregaron** (Glamorgan) was the catalyst for forming a WI. Answering an appeal from a local nursing association, a Harley Street specialist suggested the immediate formation of a WI. 'For herein lies the secret of extending to rural areas facilities which otherwise would be unavailable. Let the elder women of Tregaron gather around them the younger ones and train them in the art of keeping a good home'.

The president of **Chatteris WI** (Isle of Ely) became the town's first lady councillor.

Resolution: *This meeting urges women in England and Wales to ask for and, when possible, buy only humanely farmed furs, or artificial fur fabric, and so discourage cruelty.*

***Girton WI**, Cambridgeshire*

1932

New BBC HQ opens in Portland Place, London.

Roosevelt elected President of US, promising a 'new deal'.

• • •

Food production has always played an important role in the life of WI members and individual WI markets had been formed as early as 1916. Now, with the country suffering from economic depression and high unemployment, the need to put these markets on a more professional footing, and encourage new ones, was greater than ever.

With financial support from the Carnegie Trust, the NFWI was able to employ a marketing organiser and WI Markets was launched.

20 million eggs were still being imported into the country and egg collecting co-operatives, with neighbouring WIs, were encouraged.

Wear WI (Shropshire) sent 120 lbs of groceries and other commodities to the Royal Salop Infirmary.

Music, drama, arts and crafts were flourishing, and WIs were encouraged to take part in these activities. 'Art', reported *Home & Country*, 'in any form should not be looked upon as a luxury. It is the essence of a higher life.'

A National Handicraft Exhibition was held in London and attracted exhibits from every federation.

The NFWI set up its first NFWI Music Panel, and over 50 members from 22 WIs in **Wiltshire** took part in a Drama School.

Resolution: *That present economic difficulties render it desirable that Women's Institute members should do their utmost to improve the quality and quantity of foodstuffs they raise, increasing the amounts offered for sale through Women's Institute co-operative markets or otherwise.*

East Sussex

1933

A World Economic Conference in London draws up plans to stabilise currencies.

Hitler becomes Chancellor of the German Reich.

• • •

A motion in the House of Commons, which debated, 'That the encouragement of rural industries and the maintenance of a thriving and contented village life together with a prosperous agriculture are vital to this country', seemed to sum up the main purpose of the organisation at the time.

Many ways were suggested to members in which they could help to alleviate unemployment. These included co-operation in the Allotments Scheme, formation or support for the local unemployed in furniture repair, netting for fruit bushes, rug-making and handing on skills useful in later employment.

Mrs Alfred Watt had long dreamt of an international organisation representing the concerns of countrywomen, and with the founding of the Associated Countrywomen of the World (ACWW), in Stockholm, her dreams were finally realised. A way was now open for members to become more involved in the issues facing women in the wider world.

Barns Green & Itchingfield WI (West Sussex) organised a scheme to train six men from 'destitute areas' for farm work, and a **Northumberland** Marketing Scheme 'enabled unemployed men to dispose of their garden produce'.

A *teller* reported the Welsh conference as 'a bit mad' and said that she 'couldn't control the chairman', who was Mrs Alfred Watt!

Resolution: *That this meeting calls upon all Women's Institute members to support efforts in their own locality to deal with unemployment and distress upon both men and women.*

NFWI Executive

1934

First pedestrian crossing in London.

Mao Tse-tung's *long march* from SE China to the mountainous NW.

• • •

The NFWI continued its involvement in international affairs and reaffirmed its belief in the League of Nations. Nancy Tennant, chairman of the International Committee, spoke on behalf of the WI at the Peace Demonstration in Brussels.

The NFWI approached the government about membership of the newly established Consumers' Committee of Great Britain and three WI members were appointed to it.

WIs were encouraged to include, 'the important question of building up strong bodies, especially the bodies of children', in their programmes.

Were WI presidents holding on to office for too long in 1934? A report stated that, 'Democracy must go hand in hand with good leadership. No Institute should rely too much on its officers or on the continuance in office of trusted friends'!

Durham went on a day trip to the Norfolk Broads and Yarmouth. Members boarded the train around 3am, returning home at daybreak! There were two sittings for breakfast (6am and 7am) and for dinner (10pm and 11pm). Whist was played on the train.

A party at **Shottlegate & District WI** (Derbyshire) was enjoyed by 73 children, who all went home with a cracker, a toy, an orange and a bag of sweets.

The bird song imitations of the speaker at **Findon WI** (West Sussex) were so natural that the birds joined in!

Resolution: *Members welcome any scheme providing a milk ration for school children and urge that schools in rural areas should be given equal consideration with town schools.*

NFWI Executive

1935 – 1944

Evacuees

Travelling to a group meeting in wartime

1942 School for Produce Guild leaders

'To my mind the greatest achievement of the Institutes is that we have learned to govern ourselves. We do not believe in dictators, we believe that each member should be responsible for her Institute and should have a share in the work. It may be as a member of committee; it may be as one of those responsible for the entertainment; it may be as a helper at tea, or as a steward arranging the meeting. But the many jobs that have to be done in the perfect Women's Institute are shared by the members and not undertaken by one or two super-women.'

Lady Denman

Sorting fruit

Mobile canning van

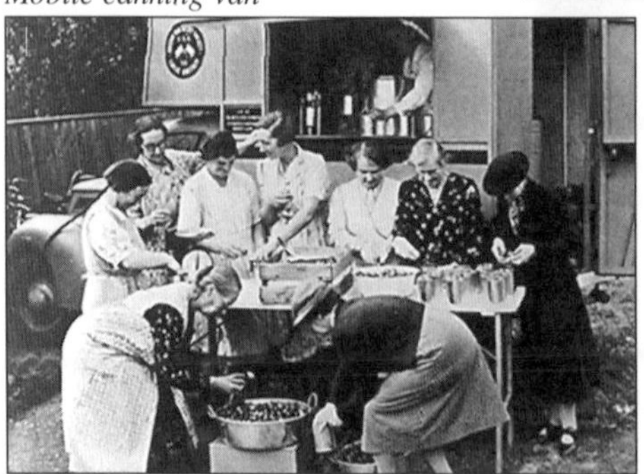

Jam centre

The rule is ...'Jam yesterday, jam tomorrow — but never jam today.'
from Lewis Carroll's 'Through the Looking Glass'.

In 1940 there were 291,000 members.

1935

30 mph speed limit introduced in built-up areas.

Mussolini invades Abyssinia.

• • •

The WI has always stressed the importance of nutrition and a healthy diet, and the NFWI held a conference in London on nutrition, attended by federation representatives, County Council instructors and experts in food values and child feeding. Following this, courses in nutrition were held in many federations. In **Durham**, where problems of unemployment were particularly acute, WIs helped to run nutrition and cookery classes in nearly a hundred villages.

The NFWI held a conference on international affairs to keep members informed of world events, then followed it up with articles in *Home & Country*.

The suggestion that WIs might be linked together for the AGM was first made at the consultative council meeting held in Stratford's Memorial Theatre.

Lady Ashton, opening **Lancashire**'s grand pageant, *Pedlar's Ware*, and Handicraft Exhibition spoke of the 'power and energy, brightness and comfort that the WI has brought into the lives of hundreds and thousands of village homes'.

Wymondham WI (Leicestershire & Rutland), supported by the Milk Publicity Council, organised a milk bar at the Melton Show, hoping to stimulate the demand for milk. And over 100 members attended three one-day poultry classes in **West Sussex**.

Cheshire organised its first county trip — a day visit to Edinburgh — and 77 members from nine WIs entered **Middlesex**'s tennis tournament.

Resolution: *WI members 'to urge Local Authorities ... to carry out the Minister's recommendations for the provision of specialised obstetric advice and an improved midwifery service.'*

Berkshire

1936

Death of George V leads to the Abdication Crisis.

Civil War in Spain.

• • •

The vexed question,'What is political and what is party political?' was discussed during a conference on International Work. It was recognised that an understanding of other nations was vital to peace, and peace was vital to all members of the nation. Members were given practical ways in which their WIs could promote better international understanding.

In a speech to the British Association, Sir Richard Livingstone, a keen advocate for Adult Education, said,

> 'There is in the WIs that social and corporate element which exists in a residential university, and which both educates and makes education attractive'.

The evening before the AGM, delegates and visitors were invited to an Annual Dinner and Reception, followed by a Dramatic Entertainment, at a cost of 6s 6d!

A note to VCOs in April's *Home & Country* states, 'The Institute offers to every woman in the village an opportunity to develop her powers of mind and heart in the service of her fellow members and of the community as a whole'.

Loddiswell WI (Devon) had a lantern lecture on conquering Everest.

Sturminster Newton (Dorset) debated: 'Men's clothes need reforming'.

A WI market producer sent in a turkey egg, priced 3d, with the accompanying note, 'If you think the egg is too high, drop it'!

Resolution: *This meeting deplores the large-scale pollution of rivers and streams in rural areas caused by trade effluent ... and calls upon the government to initiate new legislation on the subject.*

Shropshire

1937

Coronation of King George VI and Queen Elizabeth.

The artificial fibre *Nylon* is patented.

• • •

Celebrating the official coming-of-age of the NFWI on 21st July, Lady Denman, broadcasting to 318,000 members, said,

> 'The experiences of our 21 years' work shows that we can do something to add to the happiness of the countryside. No job is better worth doing'.

Members presented her with a book which contained a decorated page from each federation, 'for her contribution to the organisation for so many years'.

Appreciating this, the government asked the NFWI to contribute evidence for its survey of family budgets, and 500 sample budgets of agricultural labourers' families were collected for the report, which appeared in 1941. A deputation from the NFWI met MPs to urge that cheap milk be provided for mothers and babies.

At a time when a *Green Belt* was planned to stop urban sprawl, at the AGM members were asked ...

> 'Are we satisfied that the beauty and value of our land is being preserved?'
>
> 'Are we content with the conditions of life in the countryside?'

A limited perception of the organisation is not new. A long-time friend of the WI, Nugent Harris, commented, 'Many men think your monthly meeting is a gossip shop. Educate them by proving that the movement is carrying out its main purpose. Tell them of the national work you are accomplishing'.

Resolution: *That this meeting is of the opinion that the teaching of plain sewing and mending should be given pre-eminence over less useful crafts.*

Wiltshire

1938

All Britons to be measured for gas masks.

Hitler annexes Austria and Czechoslovakia.

• • •

The government asked the WI to assist with preparations for the evacuation of children to the countryside in the event of war. In June, a letter was sent to all WIs, saying that it was appropriate for them to co-operate with caring for evacuees but that the monthly meetings should be run as normally as possible, 'maintaining the educational and social character' and, ' thus providing for the members a centre of tranquillity and cheerfulness in a sadly troubled world'.

Lady Denman was asked by the Ministry of Agriculture to become the honorary director designate of the Women's Land Army. The NFWI executive did not accept her suggestion that she should stand down as chairman.

Caring for the countryside has always been a concern of members and a resolution was passed at the AGM urging the government to set up a co-ordinating authority to 'deal effectively with the rapidly increasing ruination of our countryside and coast' and 'preserve wide areas of special beauty ... for the health and enjoyment of this and future generations.'

Shropshire suggested that 'County Parties and Whist Drives' should take place to entertain delegates travelling to the AGM in London!

Resolution: *This meeting, realising the significant changes which are rapidly taking place in agriculture and rural life, calls on the NFWI Executive and the County Federations to encourage WI members to study these changes and to help to adapt new conditions to old.*

Gloucestershire

1939

Outbreak of World War II.

UK farmers urged to 'dig for victory'.

• • •

In the months leading up to the outbreak of war, Lady Denman was concerned that, 'In their anxiety to help in a time of national crisis, WIs should not loose sight of their peacetime functions. .... Their efforts to improve country life should not cease'.

WIs were urged to continue their musical, dramatic, handicraft and other cultural activities, 'to relieve the strain of war' and 'maintain health, strength and good spirits in the village'.

The Produce Guild was formed and the Development Commission gave a grant of £500, 'in aid of the agricultural work of the WI', with the comment that they were 'impressed by the opportunities which the Women's Institutes offer, composed as they are of producers and consumers in rural areas, for encouraging the production and treatment of fresh food stuffs'.

The 1939-40 Year Book of the Agricultural Co-operatives stated that, 'All groups of marketing societies, with the exception of the WI market stalls, show a reduction of turnover'.

Some meetings were stopped, 'on advice from the county federation and police', but later started up again. **Solihull WI** (West Midlands) commented that, 'We all felt so much happier for being together and talking with friends once more'.

Resolution: *That in view of the importance to national health of the right feeding of children, this meeting urges the Local Education Authorities to extend and improve their existing arrangements for dinners in Elementary Schools.*

NFWI Executive

1940

War continues.

As Prime Minister, Churchill asks for 'blood, toil, tears and sweat'.

• • •

The perception of WI members as perpetual jam makers will no doubt pass into folklore but jam making and canning fruit were an essential part of the WI war effort. Recognising the ability of WI members to organise themselves, the Ministry of Food gave the NFWI a grant to administer the National Fruit Preservation Scheme. America sent 500 Dixie hand sealers (home canners), oil stoves, preserving pans and other equipment, to be distributed to WIs.

A canning machine and 1000 cans, acquired by **Huntingdon & Peterborough**, proved inadequate and the following year more machines and 10,000 cans were needed!

Through the Produce Guild, members were taught how to grow fruit and vegetables more intensively in their gardens and allotments, and fruit bushes and packets of vegetable seeds, many coming from WIs in Canada, were sold through the Guild.

1,700 WIs responded to the *Town Children through Country Eyes* survey on the conditions and habits of evacuees. The responses were later influential in providing evidence that led to the setting up of the Family Allowance paid to mothers. The Queen sent a message to members praising their 'important National Service .... including work for evacuees .... and their efforts in increasing the country's food supply.

The NFWI headquarters moved to Puddephut's Farm in Hertfordshire after persistent air attacks on London.

Novelist Virginia Woolf became treasurer of **Rodmell WI** (East Sussex).

No national resolutions *as no AGMs took place in 1940,'41,'42 or '44.*

1941

The government calls for 100,000 women to do war work.

Pearl Harbour bombed.

• • •

Although the war still continued, WI members began to involve themselves in post-war planning. The NFWI sent a memorandum to the Ministry of Works and the Ministry of Reconstruction, outlining its suggestions for education, land use and local government reform, which would make Local Authorities more democratic and 'better able to deal with local needs in accordance with local opinion'.

Lady Denman was able to represent these proposals more fully when she was appointed to Lord Justice Scott's committee, which had been given the brief of looking at building and land use, 'having regard to the well-being of rural communities and the preservation of rural amenities', when hostilities ceased. The Scott report stated that, 'Women's Institutes have undoubtedly been the chief factor in the improvement of the social life of rural women' and 'have proved the organising ability of countrywomen'.

Taking charge of the evacuees

Town Children through Country Eyes, a report based on the evacuation survey, was published by the NFWI.

Through the NFWI, **Oxfordshire** bought 1,730 packets of Sutton's seeds, and collected foxglove leaves and belladonna, from which 350,000 doses of digitalis were produced.

East Suffolk produced over 52 tons of jam, with a record 4,469 pounds from **East Bergholt WI,** and five members from **Hawkinge WI** (East Kent) made '7cwt jam and filled 7cwt of cans and a hundred bottles'!

The NFWI's agricultural department moved back to London to co-ordinate the war effort and an Ambulance Fund was launched.

1942

Government plans to make school meals permanent.

Church bells ring out for El Alamein victory.

• • •

The AGM was postponed this year after the government asked societies not to meet unless it was really necessary. Not all members were happy about this. Some felt that their voices, as women, were not being valued by their Executive!

A letter informing members that the subscription would be raised from 2s to 2s 6d (a 20% increase !) was sent to all WIs.

A report from the Consultative Council included the following advice, 'Most handicrafts are now thrift crafts but thrifty things needn't be ill-made or ugly' and 'The arts are more important than ever'. Seed packets, sent from Ontario, Canada, were given to each delegate.

Knitting became a favourite activity and **Durham** members, from wool allocated by the National Service Association, had knitted 2,223 articles for the troops by the end of the year. **Upperby WI** (Cumbria) knitted 109 pairs of socks, as well as pullovers and helmets, in six months, one member alone knitting 45 pullovers.

Surrey held a Combined Choir Festival which was enjoyed by all, although one member of the audience commented mildly that, 'With some singers the words were sometimes indistinguishable. After all, it is rather intriguing to know what the author has said as well as the composer'!

In **West Suffolk** over 40 WIs, at the request of the County Council Public Assistance Committee, undertook to staff and be responsible for Rest Centres.

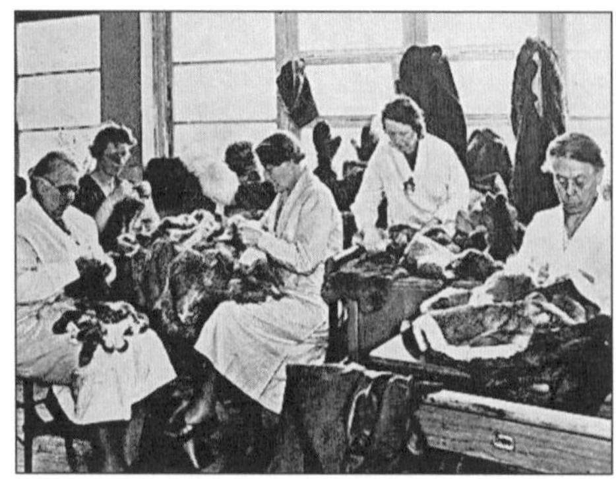

Aid to Russia fur scheme

1943

Part-time war work is made compulsory for women aged 18 to 45.

Keynes' plan for an International Monetary Fund is published.

• • •

The delegate 'linking list' was used for the first time at the only AGM held during the War. The Queen attended and delegates recorded their 'appreciation of Sir William Bevridge's work for social security and his recognition that health insurance for housewives, and children's allowances, are essential if family life is to be free from want'.

Responding to a Government White Paper on *Educational Reconstruction*, the NFWI sent a questionnaire to members asking: What kind of education do we want? 4,000 were returned. Federation conferences were held and the results of the discussions sent to appropriate government departments.

The dominant theme this year was Education, culminating in an innovative residential school in Shrewsbury, attended by 50 students from 26 counties. During the conference, Sir Richard Livingstone, prompted by Education sub-committee chairman, Adeline Vernon, and Cicely McCall, committee organiser, asked, 'Why shouldn't WIs, who have shown such remarkable common sense in their educational questionnaires, fill the Adult Education gap and provide a People's College?' The suggestion fell on fertile ground. Sir Richard's 'vision of greatness' took root and a resolution followed in 1945.

Mrs. Churchill came to the Consultative Council to thank members for supporting her *Aid to Russia* fur scheme. Members had not only made 2,071 fur-lined garments in two-and-a-half years, but had also raised the rabbits and cured the pelts!

Resolution: *That men and women should receive equal pay for equal work.*

Bures WI, *West Suffolk*

1944

Plans announced for a National Health Service after the War.

D-Day landings in Normandy.

• • •

Concerned about the lack of reasonable facilities in rural areas, the NFWI published a survey, with responses from 3,500 WIs, disclosing the horrifying conditions found in villages because of a poor water supply and lack of proper sanitation. The results were quoted in a House of Commons debate.

The NFWI, in contemplation of a move back to London after the War, bought a lease for £3,500 on 63 Chester Square, adjacent to 39 Eccleston Street, doubling the size of the office. A proposal was made that the WI should own its own hostel. This was raised again in 1947 and finally decided against in 1949.

Post-war reconstruction continued to be discussed and NFWI representatives attended an international conference on *Freedom From Want* and paid the expenses of foreign guests from funds.

The Consultative Council met in November to discuss the subject of constitutional revision.

Members were asked to knit garments for the under-twos and **West Kent** members, asking for 'skilled knitters only', reported that each WI had knitted an average of five garments each month for six months!

An urgent appeal was made for herbs and **Berkshire WI** members combed the hills for these and wild seeds. Rose hips for Vitamin C syrup were collected and 2d per pound paid for hips which, 'should be picked on a dry day when turning from green to red'. **Monks Risborough WI** (Buckinghamshire) sent nine sacks of belladonna to Islip Health Centre.

1945 – 1954

1951 'The Country Wife' mural designed to celebrate the Festival of Britain .

An early view of Denman College

'Its self-government has taught practical democracy. Its classes and lectures have given members an opportunity to look beyond their village and beyond English shores.'

Cicily McCall

1950 Outside the Albert Hall before taking part in 'Folk Songs of the Four Seasons', composed by Ralph Vaughan Williams and conducted by Adrian Boult.

In 1950 there were 446,675 members.

1945

End of World War II

• • •

From the first suggestion of a WI college in 1943, Lady Brunner, a member of the **Oxfordshire** executive and an NFWI Executive member felt, 'It was a new and exciting challenge — just what the WI needed'. And it was largely due to her imagination, courage and tenacity that the resolution to start a college was proposed and passed at the AGM.

It wasn't all plain sailing, however, and the resolution needed strong support before members' financial and other concerns had been allayed and the vote was carried. (The member seconding the resolution was so nervous that she forgot to change out of her gardening boots!)

60 years on, it seems amazing that members, having suffered nearly six years of war and deprivation, had the persistence and foresight to take up the challenge and change the vision into reality.

Rural concerns were always high on the WI agenda and over 100 members took part in a week's residential school to discuss the topic, *The Future of the Village.*

Sponsored by the British and Canadian governments, Elizabeth (Betty) Christmas, one of the NFWI's general organisers and, later, the first warden of Denman College, visited Canadian WIs to share information and thank them for their help during the War.

Resolution: *That this meeting welcomes the suggestion of a Women's Institute college, notes with satisfaction the power to provide grants for such a purpose in the Education Act 1944 and instructs the executive committee to make the necessary arrangements.*

Oxfordshire

1946

Inaugural session of United Nations General Assembly in London.

Revolutionary new pen, the *Biro*, goes on sale.

• • •

The WI has consistently stressed the importance of food production and healthy eating, and rural areas desperately needed education in domestic economy. The NFWI, aware that this was a government priority, urged federations to recruit members for training by their Local Education Authorities. Interestingly, a note of a meeting with the Minister of Education states that, 'The personnel at the Ministry, charged with these new duties, is somewhat deeply wedded to the old regime and the old conception of Education — nor does there seem any close link with the Ministry of Agriculture'!

A letter from the **Wiltshire** federation secretary, to the NFWI, suggested that opportunities for sports and games might encourage younger women to join the WI, 'as well as older women of more vigorous pursuits who cannot quite find their level among intellectual or handicraft interests. It would help to remove the occasional criticism that WIs consist of ageing members which, though far from justified, does contain a grain of truth.'

A Sports and Games sub-committee was formed the following year.

Members gave demonstrations at the *Craftswomen at Work* exhibition, held in Leamington, and the Queen attended the final of the *National Festival of Combined Arts* in London.

Resolution: *That this meeting views with grave concern the world shortage of food and pledges itself to do everything in its power to increase home production and preservation.*

Lancashire

1947

Creation of India and Pakistan as separate states.

US plane breaks the sound barrier.

• • •

With the purchase of Marcham Park, the WI's own college became 'a fact'. A £60,000 appeal for the purchase, equipment and endowment of the college had been launched the previous year and the Carnegie Trust had promised £20,000. Work could now start on making the accommodation fit for students, with Lady Brunner insisting on comfortable well-sprung beds. A conference of 'interested parties' discussed the first year's programme and the following year Denman College opened.

Helped by the Carnegie Trust, the NFWI began to form WIs in the Channel Islands and, at the end of the year, there were eight, with a membership of 407.

A residential school on *The Child*, held at Liverpool University, attracted members, 'with experience as magistrates, teachers, welfare workers, nurses and youth leaders'.

Diversity of opinion is one of the WI's great strengths and Lady Albermarle stressed this at the Consultative Council saying, 'Members work together for common aims. There can obviously not be unanimity of opinion but there can, and should, be a concord of goodwill'.

Ightham WI (West Kent) hosted a party of 26 Norwegian teachers.

Resolution: *That in the future planning of villages, thought should be given to the needs of doctors and their surgery patients. It is considered essential that each village should have either a surgery, with waiting-room, or adequate conveyance to and from the new clinics which are to be built in the towns.*

Nutley WI*, East Sussex*

1948

NHS begins 'care from cradle to grave'.

Mahatma Gandhi is assassinated.

• • •

Opening Denman College, Sir Richard Livingstone said,

> 'Education is not just schools or schooling. Its purpose is to assist us to do the things we want to do and cannot do without help — to read books, enjoy music and art, grow flowers or vegetables well, decorate a house, do needlework, bring up children, understand engines or the stars, or the laws of health and much else. We discover new interests and needs in later life and want help to pursue them. That is where a place like Denman College comes in, where one can widen one's horizons and let light into one's mind.'

Following the AGM, a preview was arranged for 750 delegates to visit the college, and 24 coaches left London in groups of three, at half-hourly intervals, in an operation christened *Movement Frolic* by the WI husband who organised it!

A National Produce exhibition was held, highlighting and publicising the excellent work of the Produce Guild, which, at a time when the cost of living was high, was encouraging members to grow vegetables to produce nourishing and appetizing meals.

At the request of the Foreign Office, the NFWI organised a three-week tour for 10 German women from the Landfrauenvereine.

Resolution: *That this meeting urges the government to introduce legislation to carry through the recommendations with regard to public footpaths, as outlined in the report of the committee on 'Footpaths and Access to the Countryside'.*

***Cambo WI**, Northumberland*

1949

Clothes rationing ends.

Mao Tse-tung declares China a Communist Republic.

• • •

The value of the relationship between the local WI and its Federation and the NFWI has been questioned since the start of the organisation. A letter from Lady Denman states, 'I am convinced that Institutes do not appreciate that their strength lies in the fact that they work together through the NFWI and the County Federations. Every conference at Denman College should strive to bring this point home'.

'There is no such thing as an associate member, only a full member,' wrote the NFWI in response to a query from a **Cornish** member, who had enquired about associate and junior membership. 'Advice on the running of Junior Clubs used to be given in the handbook but has not been included since 1936.' However it was noted that **Essex** still ran Junior Clubs.

Huntingdon & Peterborough, **Cambridgeshire** and **Isle of Ely** members visited Denmark in May and then enjoyed a reciprocal visit in September.

The first WI on the **Isle of Man** was formed and the float of five-month-old **St Andrews WI** (Guernsey) won the 'Prix d'Honneur' in the Liberation Day cavalcade, with the slogan, 'Women can make it'.

Perranuthnoe & District WI (Cornwall) lobbied for proper sanitation in rural schools and **Northamptonshire** for extra cheese rations for all workers in heavy industry.

Resolution: *That owing to the compulsory raising of the school-leaving age the authorities be requested to extend the 'half fare' travel concession to that age instead of terminating it at 14 as at present.*

Jarvis Brook WI*, East Sussex*

1950

Petrol rationing ends in Britain.

North Korea invades South Korea to start the Korean War.

• • •

Folk Songs of the Four Seasons was the highlight of the year. Over 21,000 members took part in the area rounds of this cantata, specially written for the WI by Ralph Vaughan Williams. Leading conductor, Adrian Boult, conducted 3000 members in the Royal Albert Hall.

City & Guilds invited the NFWI to set up an exploratory committee to review schemes involved in the education of agricultural workers because they were 'fully aware of the notable contributions which have already been made by a number of organisations, among which the NFWI has been outstanding'.

Guernsey and Jersey asked to be affiliated to the NFWI as 'the formation of Institutes has been an unqualified success' and WIs had quickly 'become absorbed into the lives of the islanders'. However, a cause for concern was whether or not to vote on resolutions unconnected with the islands. The diplomatic answer from the NFWI was that it was up to them, but that many WIs in England and Wales voted on resolutions on which they agreed in principle but which didn't affect their region, 'as a demonstration of support for WIs directly affected'.

The NFWI consulted WIs on the conditions and needs of rural communities.

Resolution: *That this meeting, while fully realising the difficulties of the nursing staff, deplores the fact that in some hospitals mothers and fathers are not permitted to visit their children and asks hospital management committees to allow visiting, in agreement with doctors and sisters.*

Hampshire

1951

An independent report states that the average housewife works 75 hours a week.

First H-bomb tested.

• • •

The Festival of Britain was celebrated with great enthusiasm by members. Pageants, festivals and handicraft exhibitions were held throughout the country and many members offered free hospitality to the ACWW members visiting the festival. Probably the favourite exhibit for members was *The Country Wife* mural, designed for the Country Pavilion by Constance Howard and later presented to Denman College by the government. WI members had helped to create this mural, which depicted a complete village and included many traditional WI activities.

A WI 'Ideal' House, built according to current building regulations for council houses so that it would be 'a practical possibility and not a fairy-tale house', was shown at the Ideal Home exhibition.

During her visit to Australia in its Jubilee Year, Lady Albermarle said that, 'We should use our organisation to understand national and world problems. ... There are no longer any barriers between countrywomen of the nations.'

Lady Brunner suggested that courses at Denman should 'point out that one Institute can do nothing but 7000, united through County and National Federations, can do much' and, coincidentally, **Barnack WI** (Huntingdon & Peterborough) adopted the motto, 'Together we can do that which alone we cannot do'.

Resolution: *Minister of Health urged to give greater priority to research into the causes of rheumatism, to the treatment and rehabilitation of rheumatic cases ... drawing special attention to the difficulties of country dwellers ... and increasing the number of mobile physiotherapy units in country areas.*

Nottinghamshire

1952

All-Party support in House of Commons for equal pay for women.

Albert Schweitzer wins Nobel Peace Prize.

• • •

Working with the Colonial Office and the British Council, the NFWI had regularly passed on the valuable work done by WIs in their local communities, to students from abroad. The importance of the WI in national life was recognised when the Malayan government invited the NFWI to lend them an organiser for six months, to start a WI movement in that country. Margaret Herbertson 'flew out, armed with basic visual aids on child care, hygiene, gardening, plain sewing and toy-making'.

41 members from **Berkshire**, **Yorkshire** and **Sussex** (including two husbands) were welcomed to the Netherlands by members of the Dutch Countrywomen's Association (Bond van Plattelandsvrouwen). Important international links were made and, with hospitality from members, the total cost of the twelve day visit was £8 for the fare and meals *en route* plus an additional £11!

A co-operative embroidered hanging, *The Work of Women in War Time*, now deposited with the Imperial War Museum, was exhibited at the NFWI Handicraft Exhibition held in the Victoria and Albert Museum.

The lease on 39 Eccleston Street was bought for £14,000.

At her memorial service, Mrs Nugent Harris was described as someone who gave you 'that wonderful feeling of being rather better all round than you thought you were'.

Resolution: *That this meeting, remembering that our young Queen has duties as a wife and mother, urges the nation as a whole not to overwork Her Majesty.*

Lodsworth WI, *West Sussex*

1953

Coronation of Queen Elizabeth 11.

Conquest of Mount Everest by Hillary and Tensing.

• • •

Lady Brunner's message to the Queen, from WI members, pledged 'to uphold and honour the Crown which rests today on the head of a young and lovely Queen'.

A member from **Llanfair Waterdine WI** (Powys Radnor) organised her WI's Coronation entertainment while her husband, Colonel Hunt, led a successful expedition up Everest!

At the AGM, Lady Brunner thanked the many Commonwealth countries that had donated money to the villages that had suffered from the floods in January. The guest speaker stressed the important part that WI members must play in a changing world.

Home & Country, in its report on the AGM, stated, 'First, let me reassure you: we were not knitting in the Albert Hall as reported by a usually sober daily newspaper!' Nothing changes!

Having previously successfully urged that places should be available for girls as well as boys, **Berkshire** members visited, and were shown round, a local Farm Institute.

At the Ideal Home Exhibition in March, WI Markets had a very successful stall, described by the Manchester Guardian as the best thing in Olympia. Produce included 'fruit and vegetables stored through the winter, salads brought on under cloches, spring flowers, alpines, cacti, honey, vinegars, jams, bottled fruit, sausages, pickles, poultry and eggs'.

Resolution: *This meeting urges Women's Institutes to do all in their power to encourage parents and guardians to allow their children to remain at school to complete the full educational course.*

Berkshire

1954

All rationing finally ended.

US National Cancer Unit claims definite link between cancer and cigarette smoking.

• • •

Responding to questions about the subscription in *Home & Country*, the national treasurer wrote, 'Let us remember all we get ... the position of respect and trust our Movement and ourselves have in the life of the country. One part of the Movement cannot function without the other two. Our united support is needed to build Jerusalem'.

'The thread of idealism that runs through the organisation,' a county music adviser suggested, 'can often be reinforced by music. I always hope that WIs will allow this light to shine outside their own Institute as well as inside'.

Questions asked at **East Kent**'s *Home & International* event included town planning, water supply, education, village history and records.

A founder member of **Ford WI** (Hampshire) recalled her WI as filling a gap after the death of a friend and the departure of her sister and family abroad.

> 'For two hours a month it gives me the chance to get out from behind my apron, dress up, with earrings on and a hat, and be off for a chat of matters local and entertaining, informative talks, and outings to many enlightening places.'

A light-hearted play, *Husbands are a Problem*, entertained the members of **Llanfawr WI** (Anglesey)!

Resolution: *This meeting requests the NFWI executive committee to inaugurate a campaign to preserve the countryside against desecration by litter of all kinds and urges every member of the Women's Institute to make it a personal matter to mitigate this evil.*

Northumberland

1955 – 1964

The WI at life-saving practice.

All the family take supplies to a WI market.

Rural services, such as public telephones and footpaths, have improved over the years thanks to WI campaigns.

'One thing that has always struck me is what very sensible people the original founders of the movement were. They had great foresight.'

Meriel Withal, General Secretary

'For me, the Women's Institute Movement — creating an alternative female cultural space ... campaigning to improve their material well-being and constantly challenging the socially constructed boundaries of femininity — offers an empowering tradition, a very suitable past for women today.'

Maggie Andrews

The Keep Britain Tidy campaign in action.

In 1960 there were 444,737 members.

1955

Death of Albert Einstein.

The city of London becomes a smokeless zone.

• • •

The AGM was initially postponed owing to a national rail strike and the NFWI hoped to hold it later. However the Albert Hall could only offer 23rd June and, as there was no guarantee that the strike would end, even if arrangements could be made at such short notice, it was cancelled.

Following the resolution on litter passed the previous year, the NFWI, with representatives from 20 organisations, formed the Keep Britain Tidy Group (KBTG). Although unsuccessful in its search for funding until 1958, the NFWI executive decided to work within existing resources. Lady Brunner became KBTG's first chairman and it was based in the NFWI office until 1961 when it became independent and moved to Brighton.

Following earlier surveys in 1943 and 1949, a third survey of the amenities villages should expect to have was circulated to WIs. The responses provided substantial evidence, which eventually stirred the government and local authorities into taking action.

Education in its broadest sense has always been a major aim of the organisation and Produce Guild members visited gardens and estates 'so that members can, with real knowledge, influence local authorities and others to plant and preserve our trees'.

Guernsey was addressed by Lady Dyer on 'What do we know about men?' and the remark that 'Women's Institutes are becoming too powerful' was overheard on the **Isle of Man**!

Wolverley WI (Worcestershire) lobbied for, and got, a resident policeman in their village.

***No national resolutions** were passed this year as the AGM was cancelled.*

1956

The Suez Crisis.

The Hungarians revolt against Soviet domination.

• • •

The NFWI has always worked closely with government departments and has responded to many government White Papers and consultation documents over the years. In response to a report from the Ministry of Agriculture on *Toxic Chemicals in Agriculture – Risks to Wildlife*, the NFWI stated that, 'As country women, concerned with the development and improvement of the countryside, we need to be assured that any changes will bring more beneficial than harmful results'.

Denman College held a course on *Science and Ordinary People* for 'county committee members and VCOs, and others who are prepared to stimulate interest in the subject in their counties'. Lectures covered the peaceful uses of atomic energy, chemistry and electricity. The NFWI was made an honorary corporate member of the British Association for the Advancement of Science. Four inter-county science conferences were held but members didn't really take Science up seriously until the 1990s.

West Kent members adopted families in the Funkturm Camp for Displaced Persons in Hamburg and sent them materials for curtains, sewing aids, wool and knitting needles, toys and sweets.

At the memorial service for Elizabeth (Betty) Christmas, the first warden of Denman College, she was described as 'one of those rare spirits that leave an abiding mark on all they touch.'

Resolution: *This meeting urges LEAs and governing bodies to encourage head teachers to give full consideration to the preparation of children for their duties and responsibilities as parents.*

West Kent

Betty Christmas

1957

Treaty of Rome creates the Common Market.

First Premium Bond prize-winner announced.

• • •

The NFWI held a Drama Festival over the Summer which culminated in a performance, at The Scala theatre in London, of the cycle of five verse plays, entitled *Out of this Wood* and written by the renowned poet and biographer Robert Gittings. Members, initially reluctant to 'abandon the unchallenging popular one-act plays that dominated previous drama festivals', soon overcame their reservations and discovered 'fresh and wider powers in themselves' and 'new values in drama'.

A **Kemsing WI** (West Kent) member expressed concern, in a letter to the NFWI, at the problems facing working mothers. Not wanting members to appear as 'old fogies living in the past', she wrote in *Home & Country* that, 'The challenge for us all is to help the modern woman discharge her timeless responsibility to future generations and, at the same time, find fulfilment in work both for herself, her family and the community'.

Following on from the *Science and Ordinary People* conference at Denman College, a speaker at a meeting of **Cardiganshire** members said that, 'The ideal education consists of a balance between Science and the Arts'.

Resolution: *This meeting welcomes the report of the committee of inquiry into the Export of Live Cattle to the Continent for Slaughter and urges the government to carry out the recommendations to alleviate unnecessary suffering, but is of the opinion that slaughter before export is the only real safeguard for these cattle.*

West Suffolk

1958

March of the Campaign for Nuclear Disarmament from London to Aldermaston.

First motorway in Britain— the M1 from London to Birmingham.

• • •

Implementing a resolution passed in 1957, WI members visited Fulbourne Mental Hospital, **Cambridgeshire**, with a view to forming a WI. As a WI within a hospital didn't fit with the rule that WIs be 'formed only in a village or town under 4,000 and rural in character' a 'special dispensation' was granted by the NFWI and a pilot scheme was started.

Staff, patients and ex-WI members were among the 47 members enrolled at the first meeting and the committee was elected by secret ballot from patients and staff. The matron was the president and the deputy matron the secretary, ably assisted by a patient 'who has become so enthusiastic that she has requested to attend evening typing classes'.

It was completely self-supporting, provided valuable social contact for long-stay women patients and was a two-way educative and social process for patients and the wider community.

Famous flower 'decorator', Constance Spry, judging the Flower Show at Denman College, stressed the therapeutic value of growing and arranging flowers.

A small boy wrote to Denman College, 'You gave me a lovely time camping. And you gave Mum a lovely time too. PS ... Please write and tell me if we can come back next year'.

Resolution: *That this meeting urges the appropriate Ministries to take immediate practical action to improve all inadequate sewerage systems with a view to preventing the pollution of our watercourses and seashores.*

Southerndown WI*, Glamorgan*

1959

Castro proclaims new government for Cuba.

Launch of the Mini car.

• • •

This was World Refugee Year and its purpose was to solve, once and for all, one of the world's worst social problems — the Refugee camps. WIs and federations raised almost £75,000. Many 'adopted' refugee families and some even whole camps, continuing their support for several years.

The WI's *Adult Activities* stand, presented by **Hertfordshire and Surrey**, at the *Education and Careers* exhibition at Olympia, attracted a great deal of attention.

At the Handicraft exhibition in **Durham**, members were told by Lady Dyer that, 'The WI has a great responsibility to keep crafts alive. Tradition and character must change with the times but there is room for us to keep all these crafts and alter them to suit the day'.

Following the passing of the resolution on Foot & Mouth disease at the AGM, the Minister of Agriculture urged WI members, as 'very powerful people', to 'shop around' to keep farmers, food manufacturers and shopkeepers on their toes.

Holland Moor WI (Lancashire) urged its local council to send out more anti-litter posters.

Adelaide Hoodless's granddaughter attended the AGM and the Queen visited **Stoney Creek** in Ontario, Canada, where she met the remaining founder members of the first WI.

Resolution: *That this meeting urges the Minister of Agriculture, Fisheries and Food to give nation-wide publicity to the danger of the spread of Foot & Mouth disease by the indiscriminate disposal of uncooked bone and offal.*

***Rattery WI**, Devon*

1960

In Ceylon, Mrs Bandanaraika becomes the world's first woman Prime Minister.

End of National Service in Britain.

• • •

The withdrawal or lack of transport in rural areas has always been a concern and WI members responded to a consultation paper from the government's committee on Rural Bus Services. They asked for adequate bus services to take people to shops, and welfare and medical services, and that County Transport committees be set up by those with local knowledge. **East Sussex** members discussed local transport difficulties on television.

Launching *Denman College Year* at the AGM, Lady Anglesey said that its aims were to raise a special Denman College fund, of not less than £25,000, for investment purposes, to make the college better known to members and encourage greater support.

A memo from the NFWI concerning the ACWW conference in Malaya stated that, 'In 1959 we submitted evidence to the government's Youth Service committee and are co-operating with the Duke of Edinburgh's Award Scheme for Girls by offering to arrange for WI members with special skills, to help the candidates'.

From as early as 1927 the WI had been lobbying the government for all villages to have telephones, and for rentals to be uniform throughout the country, and this year the principle was finally agreed by the Post Office.

Resolution: *That this meeting is gravely concerned at the risks associated with the use of highly poisonous sprays, insecticides and weed-killers, and urges the government to exercise more stringent control over their use.*

Cookham WI*, Berkshire*

1961

Russian Yuri Gagarin becomes first man in space.

Contraceptive pill goes on sale in the UK.

• • •

In November the NFWI sent a circular to all WIs encouraging them to support the *Freedom from Hunger* campaign (FFHC) which would be launched in 1962. During the five-year campaign members raised £185,000 and supported many international, educational, agricultural and health projects. 5% of the funds went to the UK committee to help with administration and publicity.

'One of the greatest pleasures of our WI membership is that, whatever our age, we keep looking forward, learning and planning new and better things,' declared the national chairman at the AGM. Attending the meeting, Princess Alexandra, a WI member, commented on the 'immense value and importance of this great organisation' and the benefit brought to local communities 'by the resolutions debated and discussed'.

268 members entered the NFWI's playwriting competition, for 'those whose work had not been published or performed'.

Having deplored 'the ambiguity of many recent resolutions' in 1960, **Worcestershire** members this year urged that all footpaths be 'sinposted'!

The Kremlin sent a 'cordial invitation' to Gabrielle Pike, the newly elected chairman, 'to visit the Soviet Union with a friend'.

The husbands of members of **Cowley WI** (Middlesex) formed a panel to answer questions about their thoughts on the WI. One husband considered that he now no longer 'came first'!

Resolution: *That this meeting of the NFWI pledges support to the five-year Freedom from Hunger campaign.*

Cornwall

1962

Cuban missile crisis ended after Russia agreed to withdraw.

First *Panda* crossings in London.

• • •

The NFWI launched the Karamojo Project in Uganda, in support of the *Freedom From Hunger* campaign. Its aim was to establish and equip a Farm Institute and, by showing the benefits of a well-run agricultural community with its own water supply, help to educate the younger members of the tribe, encourage conservation and raise awareness of the problems caused to the land by over-grazing and erosion. There were difficulties along the way, with marauding tribes and machinery that broke down, but Joan Yeo, former member of the National Executive, reporting on her visit to the project in 1963, said, 'I am confident that in spite of administrative difficulties, the Farm Project will eventually meet a real need'.

WI Markets raised £3000 to build and equip a trading store in Bechuanaland (Botswana). This proved to be 'a means for marketing and distribution of produce, and channelling the profit from trading back to the neighbourhood' and 'a local community centre through which the life of everybody is enlarged'.

The NFWI held a Country Feasts and Festivals competition at the Dairy Show.

Criccieth WI (Caernarfon) persuaded the Royal train to stop at Criccieth station for a photocall with the Queen, who was on her way to Pwllheli.

Resolution: *In view of the potential dangers of radiation to future generations this meeting urges the NFWI to combine with other women's organisations throughout the world in order to persuade all governments to reduce experimental nuclear explosions in the atmosphere to an absolute minimum.*

***Fetcham Afternoon WI**, Surrey*

1963

President Kennedy is assassinated in Dallas.

Beatlemania grips London.

• • •

'What really interests the woman of today and how can you include those interests in your next year's work?' was the question asked at the AGM and a conference, concerning WIs and Rural Home Economics, encouraged 'training to meet the needs of today'.

The NFWI reported to the Ministry for Agriculture, Fisheries and Food (MAFF) on Toxic Chemicals in Agriculture and Food Storage and asked that 'an obligatory statement of all chemicals in foods, called by their correct names, be added to the containers or wrappers'.

John Betjeman opened the first NFWI Art Exhibition, *Painting for Pleasure*. Keen to submit entries during a snowy winter, intrepid members carried pictures to regional exhibitions on foot, and by tractor and jeep. One excited member said that she 'had never felt more alive'.

Supporting National Nature Week and problems facing the red kite, two pictures of 'this noble bird' were presented to Denman College for the Welsh bedroom, by WI members from Cardiganshire and Carmarthenshire.

Great & Little Coxwell WI (Berkshire), instrumental in providing a local bus shelter (mainly built by husbands), urged its district council to get two lay-bys constructed, with litter-bins.

A **Bishop's Hull WI** (Somerset) member handed on her sign language interpreting skills to police cadets.

The Queen and Queen Mother encouraged fellow members at **Sandringham WI** (Norfolk) in their work for *Freedom from Hunger*.

Resolution: *This meeting draws the attention of the government to the severe shortage of physiotherapists, radiographers, occupational therapists etc. in the NHS and urges the government to offer better financial and other inducements.*

Burstow WI*, Surrey*

1964

Dorothy Hodgkin becomes the first Englishwoman to win the Nobel Prize for Chemistry.

New town of Milton Keynes conceived.

• • •

'What future for the WI?' seemed to be the theme for the organisation this year. At the Consultative Council meeting members were urged not to lose 'the spontaneity and freedom essential to voluntary work. The conscious search for a new vision and new fields to conquer can well defeat the aim of revitalising the movement and attracting the younger women of today. Monthly meeting programmes are very important. Younger women want discussions on live and controversial issues. In the fun and friendship of the WI meeting, and the opportunities it offers, are often found the springboard to further community efforts'.

WI presidents were asked 'to find exciting new ideas and discard the old, to make further use of our vast untapped collective energy' and to support the organisation financially as they had done in World Refugee Year.

Following the national chairman's visit to Russia in 1962, and a visit in 1963 to Denman College by the chairman of the League of Polish Women, Sylvia Gray, national vice-chairman, and Hilda Jones, studies' secretary at Denman College, visited Poland, to develop greater understanding with rural women.

Five WI choirs from the **Isle of Man** competed in the Manx Music Festival's special WI class.

Resolution: *That the NFWI urges the government and the Regional Hospital Boards to treat as a matter of urgency the provision of comprehensive facilities for routine smear tests for cervical cancer.*

***Whitchurch on Thames WI**, Berkshire*

1965 – 1974

A Carribean family wearing clothes made from material sent by the WI.

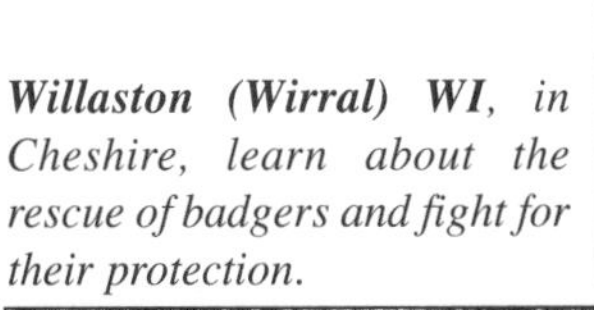

***Willaston (Wirral) WI**, in Cheshire, learn about the rescue of badgers and fight for their protection.*

Car maintenance

***Coldharbour WI** (Surrey) fought long and hard for its post bus.*

'Once I joined the WI I felt an accepted member of a very large family, with firm and secure roots and spreading branches — a stability and security which is often lacking in society today.'

Young member, 1979

'I am concerned at the *image* we have and, while it is true this is a label pinned on by a prejudiced public, many members fail to promote the better side of the WI — the serious work, the high standard and the tremendous involvement in community work.'

Another young member, 1979

'The real effect on most members isn't the large events but the many chances that are offered to widen our horizons, to learn new skills and often to gain the confidence to go out into the public arena and offer to others the knowledge gained through the WI.'

A member

Highlight of the WI's Golden Jubilee year was when members met the Queen at the Buckingham Palace garden party.

In 1970 there were 436,002 members.

1965

First woman High Court Judge appointed in this country.
Unilateral Declaration of Independence by Rhodesia.

• • •

The highlight of the WI Golden Jubilee celebrations was the Buckingham Palace garden party, attended by 9,000 members representing every WI. Throughout the year, trees, shrubs, plants and bulbs were planted in thousands. The BBC broadcast *The Countrywoman's Voice* about the WI and ITV filmed *Out of the Groove* at Denman College.

WI Markets' *Golden Market Place* at the Ideal Home Exhibition had royal visitors and a member of **Platt WI** (West Kent) made 1 cwt of fudge, making a batch each day while washing up!

The theme of the AGM was *The Countryside Tomorrow* and, writing in *Home & Country*, an officer of the county Naturalists' Trusts committee stressed that, 'Women's Institutes can play a particularly important part in ensuring that the natural features of their village, and the wild flowers, birds and animals which go with them, are not despoiled by carelessness, ignorance, misuse or simply neglect'.

At *The Countrywoman Today*'s exhibition, the entries were so good that the public didn't believe it was the work of WI members. Notices had to be put up stating that the entries were all members' own work.

The government gave grants for expenditure on Agriculture, Marketing and Crafts, and for three years £1,200 was given towards a Craft technical adviser.

Resolution: *That this meeting, while recognising our community work, urges Women's Institutes to increase their efforts for service in their own area.*

Cheshire

1966

Aberfan coal tip disaster in South Wales.

Chairman Mao launches China's 'cultural revolution'.

• • •

'If we are not consciously and constructively trying to build what we call *Jerusalem*, then we are wasting this power-house of the WI's collective energy and our movement will get hollow,' emphasised the national chairman at the AGM.

The national treasurer informed members that the organisation was facing financial difficulties. If the subscription had kept pace with inflation, it would be 14s (instead of 5s) and if it had kept in step with wages and pension increases it would be 30s.

'Our future is in your hands', she told members.

The annual report stated that the 'costs of running our WIs, County Federations and National Federation are bound to rise faster than income until such time as our subscription is adjusted to bear a much bigger proportion of those costs than at present'.

An urgent resolution, asking for £500,000 to be raised, 'to save the National Federation', was passed and the target was reached in 1969.

The NFWI had representatives on over 50 national organisations, including the Coastal Anti-Pollution League, the Keep Britain Tidy Group, the National Federation of Young Farmers' Clubs and the Food Standards Committee.

With money raised, **Glamorgan** donated 36 convector heaters, and gave food and blankets, to families living in caravans following the Aberfan disaster.

Northamptonshire held a WI Safety Day, which included driving tests, and **Bedfordshire** stressed the importance of seat belts.

Resolution: *That the NFWI should urge the government to investigate the present state of separated mothers, and the difficulties and hardship they often have in obtaining maintenance money for themselves and their children.*

Frenchay Evening WI, *Gloucestershire*

1967

Israeli-Arab six-day war.

BBC begins regular broadcasting in colour.

• • •

In conjunction with the *Freedom From Hunger* campaign, the NFWI established the Denman Rural Training Centre in Bechuanaland (Botswana). Its primary focus was short courses for village men and women, who could only leave their farms for a few days at a time, and it became so successful that it was later taken over by the Botswana government. Lady Anglesey visited projects in the Caribbean that the WI, and other organisations, had undertaken as part of the FFHC, and also a nutrition centre in Columbia to which the WI had made a financial contribution.

At the AGM, members were encouraged to get involved in their County Festivals, which formed part of the selection process for the forthcoming production of *The Brilliant and the Dark* in 1969. **Surrey** held a conference to launch its festival plans and representatives from 38 choirs turned up.

Visitors from Iran, Jordan, Botswana, Trinidad and Russia attended the AGM and the NFWI was represented at the European Movement conference and the ACWW regional conference.

WI members were urged to support Britain's first national Anti-Litter Week organised by the Keep Britain Tidy Group.

Staffordshire's Rural Community Council, working with the WI, organised a working party to look into leadership in rural areas.

'By all means let us have efficiency, but formality is not an indispensable necessity,' suggested a letter in *Home & Country*.

Resolution: *This meeting urges the government to reconsider its proposals to limit dispensing by doctors in rural areas.*

Hampton-on-the-Hill WI*, Warwickshire*

1968

Assassination of Martin Luther King in Memphis.

Theatre censorship abolished.

• • •

Having seen at first-hand children unable to go to school through lack of clothes, in co-operation with Canada's *Save the Children* fund, Lady Anglesey initiated the five-year Windward Islands clothing scheme. Sewing machines, material, buttons, threads, patterns and craft leaflets, together with WI members' letters about village life, were sent out. A letter, written when the scheme closed, confirming its value to the recipients, said, 'Their material help, as well as the stimulation received from their association and relationship with other people across the world, will long be remembered'.

A Countryside Conference was held, the Craft Design Award introduced and the Produce Show handbook published.

Visiting a local hospital, a **Surrey** member was impressed by the patients' wishes for a WI. The federation, believing that it would be difficult for the rules to be conformed to, formed the **Royal Earlswood Hospital WI** club, with the approval of the NFWI, who saw it as a 'valuable piece of community work'.

Warwickshire passed a resolution empowering its executive committee 'to investigate the possibility of forming a Housing Association to provide accommodation for WI members and other applicants'. Over 60 people were provided with accommodation during its 32 year existence.

Resolution: *That Clause 7 of the Divorce Reform Bill should include provisions granting a deserted wife, whose marriage has been terminated on the grounds referred to in this clause, financial security, tax reliefs and the pension rights of a married woman.*

Three Stones WI, *Essex*

1969

US astronauts, Neil Armstrong and Buzz Aldrin, are first men to walk on the moon.

Maiden flight of Concorde.

• • •

The triumph of the year was the performance of *The Brilliant and the Dark*, composed by Malcolm Williamson and written by Ursula Vaughan Williams. 1000 singers from 49 choirs, eight pianists, eight soloists and about 150 actors and dancers from **East Sussex** and **Hertfordshire** were on stage at the Royal Albert Hall. Depicting all aspects of life, from 1066, the musical drama contrasted the tragedies in the lives of women, caused by war, poverty and injustice, with their achievements and advancement.

Celebrating the investiture of the Prince of Wales, an exhibition, *Gwyl Gwalia*, showing the variety and many activities of the WI in Wales, was held at Plas Newydd, home of the Angleseys. Their living room was turned into a canteen for catering purposes!

'We are listened to seriously as representative of thoughtful public opinion, because we do not represent a narrow section of the community but are widely based and reasonably well informed', the national chairman informed members at the AGM. Evidence gathered from WI members helped to shape the Divorce Reform Act.

A new NFWI leaflet, *The Countryside: a Code for WIs*, was widely used by county councils and countryside organisations, and a decimal currency school was held in London for WI Market committee members.

The Appeal Fund, launched in 1966, closed with £527,777 donated 'to save the NFWI'.

Resolution: *That the WI movement exert its influence to conserve our countryside to the best advantage of the whole community.*

Mount Rayleigh WI*, Essex*

1970

European Conservation Year

First major oil find in UK sector of the North Sea.

• • •

The NFWI launched its *Town & Country* project, with £5,000 funding per annum for three years from the Carnegie UK Trust, to support a project officer. Its aim was to promote understanding between people living in rural and urban areas and help them learn more about each other's problems and priorities. In a two-way exchange, projects had to involve whole families from a range of backgrounds.

The NFWI held a conference on the Common Market in London and another, with county directors of Education and representatives of Adult Education, at Denman College, attended by the BBC and ITA.

An article by the Nature Conservancy in *Home & Country* raised concerns about the dangers of carbon dioxide build-up and melting polar ice-caps, and the editor asked, 'Could the problems of disposal and pollution created by our throw-away society become so urgent that once again there is virtue in things which last?'

The **Powys Radnor** *Field Names Project*, running to 11 volumes, won the Prince of Wales' *Countryside in 1970* award and **Strete WI** (Devon) urged its RCC not to spoil the character of its village with its local building proposals.

The Queen Mother opened the Teaching Centre and the Brunner Buildings at Denman College.

Resolution: *This meeting is concerned that, whatever the final structure proposed for the form of local government, due provision should be made to ensure that rural views and interests are heard and acted upon.*

NFWI Executive

1971

Decimal currency introduced in the UK.

World's first heart and lung transplant operation.

• • •

At the ACWW Triennial Conference in Oslo, Olive Farquharson, past national vice-chairman, became the first Englishwoman to be elected World President.

An important constitutional resolution was discussed at the AGM, changing the interpretation of the non-party political and non-sectarian rules to include political issues. Lady Albermarle stated that greater freedom of discussion would encourage potential members and future leaders to join, and the national chairman stressed that, 'It needs courage to make change'. The resolution was passed.

The NFWI undertook a joint public relations' project with the magazine *Woman's Realm*, to promote the importance of crafts, and the entries were sold in aid of the *Save the Children* fund. Federations were asked for ideas about how inter-county sporting events could be arranged.

A *Keeping Ourselves Informed* conference, to discuss government proposals for local government, was held in London and the first concert of the WI Music Society (a spin-off from *The Brilliant & the Dark*) was given, with the Young Musicians' Symphony Orchestra.

Dorset held a conference on decimalisation and a **Devon WI** increased its membership, 'due to the friendly atmosphere which exists among the members, who come from all walks of life and are able to work well together for a worthy cause'.

Resolution: *That this meeting urges the Minister of Posts and Telecommunications to examine the problems underlying the closure of so many Sub-Post Offices, which is causing hardship in rural areas, and to take remedial action.*

Madron WI*, Cornwall*

1972

Britain joins European Economic Community.

General Idi Amin expels 50,000 Ugandan Asians to the UK.

• • •

The scene for the year's major exhibition, *This Green and Pleasant Land*, was set three years earlier by Lady Anglesey, who said that, 'We should all learn about our countryside. ... The more we learn about the problems of conservation, the more concerned we become. We need to stimulate effective action which alone can make conservation a reality'.

Heritage was the theme of *Treasures in our Midst*, the first NFWI out-of-town conference. Held in Chester, it attracted speakers from the British Museum, Ironbridge Gorge Open Air Museum and the National Museum of Wales. Another conference looked at problems in Britain, 'in the light of some experiences in Europe and other continents', and asked, 'Are we giving our children too academic an education and failing to give lessons in living?' An Open University/NFWI conference welcomed husbands and older children.

Following a mandate on nursery education, NFWI wrote to the government stressing the importance of education for the under-fives.

The Guild of Learners and the Produce Guild closed. Their activities continued under the title of Home Economics, with basic certificates available in Home Skills, Cookery, Craft and Gardening.

To educate members in road safety, **Warwickshire** suggested a national WI *Driver of the Year* competition. This eventually happened in 1990!

Resolution: *This meeting urges the government to make it mandatory rather than permissive, as at present, for all local authorities to provide a full free Family Planning service.*

Anglesey

1973

International oil crisis as OPEC raises price four-fold.

Miners' strike leads to 3-day working week in Britain.

• • •

Government departments were often represented on NFWI sub-committees and proved mutually beneficial. 'The NF does value the services of your representatives very highly', wrote the NFWI general secretary to MAFF in May. 'I have enjoyed my three years with you and only wish I had more time to follow up the many interesting developments', said the department of Education & Science's representative, in August.

A spokesman from the Department of the Environment came to the NFWI's *Water, Water Everywhere* conference in London. The NFWI was affiliated to *Transport 2000* and the national chairman was appointed to the UK council of *European Architectural Heritage Year 1975*.

The NFWI set up a sub-committee to organise the first Lawn Tennis Championship in which 44 federations took part. Sponsored by rose-grower, Harry Wheatcroft, the final was held at the Queen's Club in London.

A sociology student from Nigeria spent a week in **Buckinghamshire**, as a guest of the federation, studying English rural life.

A member of **Handcross WI** (East Sussex) spent 15 months, sponsored by her federation, as a VSO volunteer teacher.

In response to *Plant a Tree in '73*, **Cofton Hackett WI** (Worcestershire) mounted a campaign to protect 262 mature hardwood trees.

Resolution: *This meeting, in the interests of rural life and the environment, urges the government to formulate a comprehensive transport policy with special regard to the present disparity in expenditure on roads and railways.*

NFWI Executive

1974

First indication of problems facing the ozone layer from CFCs.

Local government reorganisation.

• • •

'Don't you think it's time we tackled some of the problems not always considered to be the province of women today?' asked the national chairman, in a year of local government reorganisation.

The NFWI held a conference on *Boundaries* and announced its decision to realign federations with local authority boundaries. Acknowledging that this would lead to problems in some areas, federations nevertheless responded well to the changes. A course was held at Denman College, 'to examine the new structure in its various aspects and consider how the individual in all walks of life will be affected by the changes, whether he or she is an active councillor or a passive citizen'.

The subscription was increased to £1, supported strongly by a pensioner who said, having recently paid just over 27p for a small pork chop, that, 'the WI provided much better value than four pork chops'.

Representatives from 50 federations attended the first NFWI Drama conference for nine years and discussed 'the progress and changing pattern of WI drama as an important recreational and educational pursuit'. Another conference looked at *Crime & Punishment.*

A recipe for *Restoration Jelly* in the reprinted NFWI booklet, *Lotions & Potions*, began, 'An infallible recipe for an old woman or a sick turkey'!

Resolution: *This meeting urges the government to institute a national policy to co-ordinate and develop the reclamation, recycling and re-use of ingredients in domestic and industrial waste.*

Chobham Evening WI*, Surrey*

1975 – 1984

WI Beefeaters get into Jubilee mood during the Romney Revels.

Clearing litter from Herne Bay, Kent, during the KBTG's Jubilee 'Clean for the Queen' campaign.

Protest marchers protect their right of way.

'When I first moved to Mid-Wales from Shropshire I was still teaching full time back in Shropshire, travelling daily, so it was difficult to get a social life started. Then I joined the WI! What a difference this made to my life.'

A member

Queen Elizabeth the Queen Mother, patron of the KBTG, and, with the Queen, a member of Sandringham WI.

In 1980 there were 384,288 members.

1975

Americans leave Vietnam.

UK says 'yes' to joining the Common Market.

• • •

In their Diamond Jubilee Year, members were urged to be 'passionate for moderation, to hang on to rational argument and common sense and to work for the good of the whole community'. And, in what was also International Women's Year, they pledged themselves to work for 'equality of opportunity and legal status for men and women'.

Inspired by Laura Ashley, a major craft exhibition entitled *Tomorrow's Heirlooms*, was held at the Commonwealth Institute. The College of Arms created a coat-of-arms for our organisation once the NFWI had established 'appropriate credentials'.

Having passed a resolution in 1972 asking for 'high priority' to be given to 'the provision of nursery education for all children', the NFWI became a member of *Fair Play for Children*. Its policy was to set up play councils throughout the country.

The NFWI, concerned about cutbacks in government provision for rural Home Economic advisory services, wrote to the Department of Education & Science. The response wasn't encouraging!

Triumphing over teams from 16 federations, **Northamptonshire** won the BBC WI Quiz and, stimulated by her success, a member went on to compete, over the years, on *Mastermind*, *Brain of Britain* and *Today's the Day*.

Resolution: *While welcoming the government's Committee of Inquiry into the problems of battered wives, this meeting urges that immediate action be taken to provide alternative accommodation for these women and their children in at least every county if not every town.*

***Barnack WI**, Huntingdon & Peterborough*

1976

Death of Mao Tse Tung.

Closure of the Elizabeth Garrett Anderson Hospital.

• • •

In the worst inflationary year since the WI began, the organisation faced financial difficulties again. Proposing the resolution that the National Executive should decide the amount and division of the subscription in consultation with the Consultative Council, **Surrey** said, 'We can sound the death knell of our organisation or give it the kiss of life'. 'Who is going to join us if it means so little to those who already belong?' asked the national treasurer. The resolution was passed and an appeal for 50p per member over two years raised over £90,000.

A TV Times/WI *Cook of Cooks* competition was held and 606 pairs entered the NFWI/Green Shield Tennis Tournament. A caller to a Radio Birmingham phone-in after the AGM asked if there was a Junior Section of the WI.

A **Siddington-with-Preston WI** (Gloucestershire) member won the NFWI/Practical Gardening competition. The competition was for a garden of a quarter-of-an-acre laid out for attractiveness and ease of management, with a practical approach to the problem of growing a balanced collection of flowers, fruit and vegetables.

Holyport WI (Berkshire) wrote a letter inviting *Gardeners' Question Time* to help celebrate its 21st birthday. The event finally took place in 2000!

Resolution: *In view of the difficulties and decreasing facilities of public transport this meeting urges that the relevant Road Traffic Acts be amended to allow for more flexibility in transport schemes in rural areas wherever necessary.*

East Sussex

1977

Queen Elizabeth II's Silver Jubilee.

Two Belfast women win the Nobel Peace Prize.

• • •

A sale of WI crafts at Debenhams, Oxford Street, raised over £42,000 for the Queen's Silver Jubilee Appeal and, celebrating the Jubilee, **Suffolk West** held a village maps' competition and the book of maps was presented to the Queen in 1979.

The WI in the Community was the theme for the Royal Show and suggested actions included looking after village halls and keeping footpaths open. **Warwickshire** gave daily *Eat British* cookery demonstrations.

Looking for European organisations on which it could be represented, the NFWI visited Brussels.

Reviewing *Jam and Jerusalem*, published during the year, a columnist wrote, 'Only a fool would mock this formidable army as it marches onward still determined to build Jerusalem in England's green and pleasant land'.

With remarkable foresight, an article in *Home & Country* asked if a flexible retirement age between 60 and 70 should be implemented, in light of the anticipated decrease in the labour force and a growing number of pensioners. A WI in **Cornwall** kept former members in touch and involved by holding an extra afternoon meeting in an old peoples' home.

With county boundary changes, the last chairman of **Lindsey** became the first chairman of **Humberside**.

A member of **Cheswick WI** (Northumberland) represented Scotland in the European Curling Championships in Oslo. The team won a silver medal.

Resolution: *This meeting urges the government to give greater priority to research into alternative sources of energy.*

***Harracot WI**, Devon*

1978

World's first test-tube baby — born in Oldham.

First crossing of the Atlantic by balloon.

• • •

'No generation has a right to squander resources to subsidise its own consumption', said a speaker at the *Energy Today and Tomorrow* conference organised by the NFWI in conjunction with other women's organisations. 'Our diminishing fossil fuels must be gradually replaced with corresponding amounts of alternative, rather than nuclear, energy,' he said. And the Prime Minister stated that, 'We should educate our children now to have a greater respect for energy than we have had'.

The NFWI began a two-year project, *Good Health is Good Fun*, in association with Kelloggs, highlighting the problems associated with obesity. In support, a **Buckinghamshire** member walked 259 miles to Liskeard in Cornwall with her black Labrador, staying with fellow members on the way.

A letter from the NFWI to the Advisory Council for Agriculture & Horticulture stated, 'We would like you to know of our interest in doing all we can to promote understanding between town and country. If there is anything you feel that a voluntary organisation such as ours could do to help in this we should be very willing to co-operate'.

The NFWI officially joined forces with the Confederation of Family Organisations in the European Community (CoFACE), thus giving it a greater and much needed consumer voice in Europe.

Resolution: *This meeting views with deep concern the dangers to marine life from over-exploitation and pollution, and urges that the effect of these should be more closely monitored and controlled internationally.*

***Brixham WI**, Devon*

1979

Margaret Thatcher becomes Britain's first woman Prime Minister.

The Shah of Iran is exiled.

• • •

The Queen opened the Home Economics centre at Denman College. Visiting some of the courses during the day, she is reported to have had 'a friendly discussion with the gardening tutor on the best time of year to prune roses'!

Questions at the NFWI/Industrial Society joint conference on *Why Industry Matters to Society* included: Should we separate waste? Why do we need new airports when oil is said to be running out and some aircraft are half empty? Why can't commuters be encouraged to share car journeys? and What about alternative energy?

Many child-related projects were undertaken by members during the International Year of the Child. The **Isle of Man** bought an incubator for a hospital's children's ward and **Devon** supported a toy library for handicapped children.

Gloucestershire, invited to help furnish the new Beatrix Potter Museum in Gloucester, took sketches of the waistcoat on exhibition in the Victoria & Albert Museum. Using old materials and threads, for authenticity, an exact replica of the one illustrated in *The Tailor of Gloucester* was made and presented to the museum.

Herefordshire started a Rounders League and the Red Devils of **Much Cowarne WI**, coached by the local barman, took on all comers!

Resolution: *This meeting ... urges the government and local authorities to restrict the closure of small schools after considering the effects, not only on the children, but on village communities as a whole.*

***Hannington WI**, Hampshire*

1980

John Lennon shot dead in New York.

WHO claims that smallpox has been eliminated as a human disease.

• • •

The drama festival, *Scene '80: A Festival of Creative Entertainment*, was the major event of the year. Following 62 countrywide festivals, members from nine federations took part in the three-day finals performed at the Royal Shakespeare Company's theatre in Stratford-upon-Avon. Donald Sinden, whose mother had been president of her own WI, was patron of the event, which aimed to illustrate and celebrate local history, folklore and customs in speech and song.

The NFWI was represented on over 70 organisations, including the Tree Council, Consumer Standards Advisory Committee, the Independent Broadcasting Authority, and the Open University Advisory Committee on Adult and Higher Education.

A conference on Nutrition was held at Denman College in the recently opened Home Economics centre.

Rampton WI (Cambridgeshire) started a medi-car scheme, which drove local elderly people to neighbouring surgeries.

Glamorgan raised £3000 to organise and support adventure holidays for under-privileged children.

West Sussex planted 600 trees on the South Downs Way and **Mold WI** (Clwyd Flint) planted oaks and beeches in its local community.

Local protests from **Ferring WI** (West Sussex), about building on open spaces, and from **Appledore WI** (Devon), against a dangerous footpath, were successful.

Resolution: *In view of the alarming increase in under-age drinking of alcohol, this meeting calls upon the government to promote more education in homes, schools and youth organisations about the danger of alcohol.*

***Cheddar Hannah More WI**, Somerset*

1981

Launch of *Columbia*, the world's first re-usable spacecraft.

Unemployment reaches 2.5 million in the UK.

• • •

Early One Morning, specially commissioned by the NFWI, with words and music written by the composer Anthony Hopkins, was performed, along with *Folk Songs of Four Seasons* (See 1950), in three prestigious venues. Written to 'represent a challenge for WI members but also with immediate appeal', *Early One Morning* described the life of women in contemporary society.

The National Council, made up of the NFWI executive committee and all federation chairmen and treasurers, replaced the Consultative Council. The Campaign for Nuclear Disarmament, in a briefing paper, misrepresented the NFWI as being an affiliated member.

Wiltshire began discussions with architects, builders and Kennet District Council about its own *WI House at the Wharf*, which was opened in 1983 at a cost of approximately £30,000.

Writing in *Home & Country*, a member urged. 'Come on you Institutes who are set in your ways; let your new members have their say and who knows what may happen'.

MPs in the Palace of Westminster enjoyed home-made jam on their scones in January, when the national chairman and members lobbied successfully for a law to be changed. A bill, making WI Market cooks exempt from having to register their kitchens with the local authority, was passed in July.

Resolution: *This meeting urges the Women's Institutes to do all in their power to maintain national varieties of fruit, vegetables and farm crops.*

***Colehill Afternoon WI**, Dorset*

1982

Argentina invades the Falkland Islands.

Greenham Common protest by 20,000 women against US cruise missiles.

• • •

With the country suffering from exceptionally high unemployment, a *Work and Leisure in the 1980s* conference was held at Denman College, with LEAs, other women's organisations and relevant national institutions, to focus attention on ways in which people could work at local level to sustain their communities and find ways of coping with increased leisure.

A **Durham** executive member and publicity officer was given an advertising slot on Tyne Tees television to talk about the opportunities offered by the WI.

Home & Country asked younger members for their views on the WI. One commented that, 'What I like about the WI is the sense of belonging and being involved. What I don't like is too much formality; I feel it puts younger women off.' And another wrote, 'My WI is very much concerned with itself rather than the organisation nationally. I'm not implying that this is a bad thing but for myself I would like to become more involved nationally – even internationally – but until I started taking *Home & Country* I found it very difficult to get to know the extent of the organisation'.

A **Gloucestershire** member ran in the London Marathon.

Resolution: *This meeting considers that public telephone kiosks in rural areas are an essential service, especially vital in emergency situations, and as such should be protected by a government subsidy if necessary, against recovery by British Telecom on commercial grounds.*

Cornwall

1983

Sally K Ride became the first woman in space.

The Walton sextuplets born in Liverpool — all girls.

• • •

Concerned about a significant drop in membership, the NFWI commissioned a Membership Survey from Strathclyde University. As a result, and to raise the profile and change the public's perception of the organisation, the *Women in the Community,* a three-pronged project, *Women and Education*, *Women and Health* and *Women in Public Life*, was launched.

Five-year funding by the Development Commission allowed *Training Adults* courses to be started in the federations, which used new training techniques.

Having consulted members, the NFWI sent a memorandum to the Warnock Committee on the legal, moral and ethical issues relating to human fertilisation and embryology, and followed this up the next year with recommendations and discussion papers. 51 federations responded.

Celebrating their Golden Jubilee, **Clwyd Flint** members created a magnificent *Countryside Collage* — a map of the area, worked in wool, illustrating the WI mandates passed between 1933 and 1983.

At a time of high unemployment, **Warwickshire** members worked with the Manpower Services Commission as agents. 58 people were employed, cleaning streets, cutting back hedges and planting trees, in its *Keep Warwickshire Tidy* initiative.

Six new federations were formed from the large **Yorkshire** federation.

The **Cranleigh Group of WIs** (West Sussex) presented 280 plants to the Prince and Princess of Wales, for the herb garden at Highgrove House, and planted them.

Resolution: *This meeting of Women's Institutes urges its members to promote and support the provision of hospice care for those patients who desire it.*

Stockland WI*, Devon*

1984

Discovery of AIDS virus.

IRA bomb blast at Tory conference in Brighton.

• • •

This was a year of promotion. A huge *Life and Leisure* exhibition was staged at Olympia, supported by the National Westminster Bank, and commercial and other exhibiters, and opened by the Queen, who stayed for two hours. The emphasis was on action and participation, and involved every federation and every sphere of activity.

The King of Lesotho visited the exhibition and was presented with a £50,000 cheque to help with water and sanitation projects, and the three year NFWI/UNICEF Maldives project was launched, aimed at providing health, education and income-generating schemes.

More publicity came from the *WI Promotion Bus*, provided free by the National Bus Company, which toured England and Wales for nine months, visiting 200 towns and cities, and from in-store promotions with British Home Stores and International Stores.

A *Milk – Use it or Lose it* leaflet was circulated to federations and the NFWI considered what action to take on the government's White Paper on Buses.

Hertfordshire had 130 applications for its Computer Day.

Lincolnshire North's participation at the National Ploughing Championships was memorable, not only for its display tent but also for the rain and the picture of WI cars being towed off site by tractors!

Resolution: *This meeting urges the government and planning authorities to ensure that full use is made of the possibilities for in-filling redevelopment and the use of derelict and waste land, before granting planning permission to develop green field sites.*

Uley WI*, Gloucestershire*

1985 – 1994

*Members from **East Bridgford WI**, Notts, complete a half-marathon.*

***Cambridgeshire**'s highly successful Medicar scheme.*

*Bus survey conducted by **Ringmer Evening WI** in East Sussex.*

'... The personal support of all the friends made over the years, through my involvement with the WI, gave me the courage to come through a very dark period and forge a new life for myself.'

A member in the 1990s

'I have, through joining the WI, been given many opportunities and have made lots of friends ... but I have a special friend who is always willing to listen and give advice when asked. To relax over the occasional cup of tea, visit the theatre or enjoy the odd day out with her is a real pleasure. If I hadn't joined the WI I wouldn't have known her. Thank you WI for my very best friend!'

A member

1988 The cottage garden which won a gold medal at Chelsea.

In 1990 there were 318,736 members.

1985

Mikhail Gorbachev becomes head of the Soviet Union.

Wembley concert for Live Aid.

• • •

'We must not allow custom and tradition to scare off new members', said the national chairman at the AGM.

New fire regulations, a design fault in Brunner House and a backlog of maintenance work threatened Denman College with closure. Federations were asked to consult their members and report back to the National Council in the Autumn. The answer came back, 'Save Denman', and an appeal for £1 million was launched to carry out necessary and urgent repairs, and provide a maintenance fund for the future.

The NFWI joined the 300 Group campaigning for more women to be involved in local government, and also campaigned with *Friends of the Earth* to save rural bus services, at a time when bus services were being de-regulated. 'Unfortunately', commented environmentalist Jonathon Porritt in 1990, 'everything we warned about has come to pass'!

Gwent members made a collage for the Royal Welsh Show, depicting the two faces of Gwent, rural and industrial, which was later sold to the Wool Marketing Board to raise money for the Denman Appeal.

With more time for leisure pursuits, members showed a greater interest in active sport and an NFWI Festival of Sport was held in York, sponsored by the Milk Marketing Board, who also supported one in Bath the following year.

More active sport also provided by the Tennis Championships.

Resolution: *This meeting urges the government to take steps now to control the emission of sulphur and nitrogen oxides from power stations in order to reduce acid rain.*

***Surlingham WI**, Norfolk*

1986

Explosion in nuclear reactor at Chernobyl.

First visit to China of British monarch.

• • •

'We have to be seen to be dynamic — a force for good and a force for change,' a speaker on *Women as Decision Makers* told members at the AGM.

The constitution was amended to include the advancement of the education of women as a purpose of the organisation and the NFWI appointed an education and training officer, and set up a new education sub-committee.

The NFWI supported the *Save Child Benefit* campaign led by the Child Poverty action group.

Celebrating the 40th Anniversary of the Wildfowl Trust, members were invited to enter a joint NFWI/Wildfowl Trust Embroidery and Collage competition.

The winning entry, *Food for All*, by **West Row WI** (Suffolk West), in the *Environment Under Attack* competition was described as 'clear, thought-provoking and practical'. Concluding that women could have a real influence through their family, education, political pressure and work, the entry illustrated the differences between Western (meat and dairy) and African (grain) diets. 12 lbs of grain — enough to feed 25 people for one day — is needed to produce 2 lbs of beef.

Staffordshire's garden won a silver medal at the National Garden Festival at Stoke-on-Trent and **Wiltshire** members helped the National Consumer Council with a pilot survey of pedestrian access in Salisbury.

Resolution: *This meeting urges its members to support the campaign of the Department of Health to inform the general public of the true facts concerning the disease AIDS.*

Crickhowel WI*, Powys Brecknock*

1987

International agreement to cut down CFCs to save the ozone layer.

Storm of the century lashes England.

• • •

A wide consultation with members resulted in a very comprehensive *WI Countryside Policy* at a time when the government was proposing radical changes in the pattern of agriculture and rural land use. It illustrated how these changes would affect rural services, conservation of the landscape, wildlife and the soil.

The NFWI supported the *Farm Safety Campaign* and, with links between health and food a continuing concern, forged new links with the Agricultural and Food Research Council.

Water-sports taster days were held at nine centres countrywide, supported by the Milk Marketing Board, and a Flower Festival was held at Denman College for members to view the improvements made there. Calor Gas donated £50,000 to the Denman Appeal.

Members of **Penstrowel WI** (Powys Montgomery) were given £1 each to raise money and one member raised £242 for local hospices using the £1 to have posters printed for her bric-a brac sale in a disused shop.

Because of the energy and enthusiasm of a **Tremont WI** (Powys Radnor) member, the first *Bottle Bank* in the county was established in Llandrindod Wells.

A farmer's wife from **Ockbrook Radhills WI** (Derbyshire) travelled to New Zealand, on a James Cook scholarship, to study its dairy industry.

Resolution: *This meeting urges the government to work with the credit industry to bring under control the aggressive and indiscriminate sale of credit, and to give more publicity to the hazards of borrowing money.*

***Filkins and Broughton Poggs WI**, Oxfordshire*

1988

Arafat declares Palestinian State.

Research shows that aspirin can reduce heart attacks.

• • •

Funded by the Equal Opportunities Commission, the NFWI held a joint conference, *Points of Change in Women's Lives*, at Denman College, with members of the Workers' Education Association. Three topics were chosen to provide the basis for future collaborative activities – Education, Public Life, and Work. WEA students commented later that, 'Having our prejudices removed was a salutary experience and one we would not have missed'. And, 'We had some disagreements but ultimately the feeling was one of growing respect and an awareness that we could help each other a great deal'.

The BBC wrote to *Home & Country* appealing for a cook to take part in the series, *The Victorian Kitchen*. This was the start of a new career for a member of **Hampstead Norreys WI** (Buckinghamshire).

Environmental campaigning continued. A **Penyfair WI** (Glamorgan) member began a campaign to save a local woodland and **Winterbourne WI** (Avon) spearheaded a campaign, with other organisations, to protect an area of great beauty in the Frome valley.

The WI cottage garden, designed by a member of **Burton & Puddington WI** (Cheshire), and created by Bridgemere Garden World, based in the county, won a Gold Medal and the Wilkinson Sword of Honour, at the Chelsea Flower Show.

Resolution: *In view of the depletion of stratospheric ozone, this meeting urges WI members to do everything in their power to discourage manufacturers from using chlorofluorocarbons (CFCs) in either products or processes and urges the government to make labelling mandatory for all products that contain CFCs.*

Corfe WI*, Somerset*

1989

Fall of Berlin Wall and collapse of Communism in eastern Europe.

'Guildford Four' released from prison.

• • •

The NFWI/UNICEF *Women in Brazil, a* joint three-year project, was launched. Its aim was to help women to help themselves, and work in partnership with local organisations so that projects would be relevant and sustainable. Members were asked to raise £30,000 and the three main areas targeted were Health, Literacy, and Skills. In 1991 a course was held at Denman College to update members and give further suggestions for involvement.

Having initially thought the resolution on toxic waste, passed at the AGM, irrelevant, members of **Matlock WI** (Derbyshire) joined a local campaign against a toxic waste tip and urged members in similar campaigns, 'to use the WI to help spread the word'.

An inspirational young president in **Acle WI** (Norfolk) decided that members would get more from the WI if they were 'more in touch nationally'. New 'ventures' included an Environment Week, a WI books library and a WI disposal scheme for newspapers and bottles.

In a message in *For Home & Country*, published to celebrate the magazine's 70th Birthday, the Queen wrote, 'The role of the WI in encouraging home skills and traditional crafts, its important work for women's health, the improvement of rural services and the safeguarding of the environment, are as important as ever today.'

The NFWI's *Action Packs* were made available for the first time.

Resolution: *The NFWI calls upon the government to introduce legislation for compulsory DNA testing in those areas where violent crime has been committed.*

Old Heathfield WI*, East Sussex*

1990

Nelson Mandela freed after 27 years in prison in South Africa.

Poll Tax uproar sweeps the country.

• • •

The NFWI's *Women in the Nineties* conference, sponsored by Marks and Spencer, attracted an impressive list of speakers. Issues discussed included: women in leadership roles; 'family friendly' policies; the pay gap; women's health; global warming; food safety and transport. Introducing the environmentalist, Jonathon Porritt, the journalist Polly Toynbee told him that, 'his best hope for the future of the environment lay with women'.

Important constitutional changes were agreed and passed at the AGM, attended by the Queen.

Celebrations to mark the WI's 75th birthday included a Federation of Wales exhibition at St Fagans, an Arts and Crafts exhibition at Rufford Craft Park, Nottingham, and an NFWI/ National Westminster Bank choir festival. On **Tyneside**, *Jerusalem*, played on the city's carillon, could be heard throughout Newcastle-upon-Tyne.

The NFWI's *Driver of the Year* competition, sponsored by Vauxhall Motors Ltd., was launched by Joanna Lumley, the newest recruit to **Goodnestone WI** (Kent), and a **South Yorkshire** finalist in the competition was inspired to enter the *Monte Carlo Dash*, a rally for women over 60, organised to raise money for an Afghan midwife project.

Suffolk West welcomed a delegation of Soviet women, all from farming backgrounds.

Resolution: *This meeting urges the government to do everything in its power to persuade other countries ... that Antarctica be declared a wilderness park within which the extraction of oil and minerals, and other commercial, polluting and military activities, should not be permitted.*

***Glemsford WI**, Suffolk West*

1991

Collapse of the Soviet Union. President Gorbachev resigns.

Terry Waite freed from captivity in Beirut.

• • •

10,000 members attended the first two-day Triennial General Meeting. This took the place of the former AGM and was held in the NEC arena in Birmingham. A brass band concert was held on the first evening and many commercial firms and charities took stands in the exhibition hall. Anita Roddick, founder of the Body Shop group, was the guest speaker.

The NFWI joined a powerful coalition of consumer and health organisations in the House of Commons to launch the Healthy Eating campaign, held in conjunction with the World Health report, which linked diets high in fats, sugars and salts (and low in fibre, fruit and vegetables) with major preventable diseases.

Following the launch of a government white paper, *Education and Training for the 21st Century*, which proposed classifying non-vocational courses as 'leisure courses' and therefore liable to VAT, the NFWI took a leading role in successfully persuading the government to reconsider its proposals. The WI campaign became a 'cause célèbre' in adult educational circles.

The *Healthy Eating Takes Some Beating* day, held by **Dyke WI** (South Lincolnshire), in a local primary school on election polling day, showed that it was possible to feed children well, easily and cheaply, and it also attracted new members.

Resolution: *This meeting urges that more publicity be given to the dangers of proprietary drugs containing paracetamol which, if taken in excess, may lead to renal/liver damage and possible death.*

Lymm WI*, Cheshire*

1992

Civil War erupts in Bosnia.

***Annus horribilis* for the Queen, including fire at Windsor Castle**

• • •

Science, the environment and the pursuit of knowledge were much in evidence this year.

60 federation representatives took part in a science conference, sponsored by COPUS, which included discussions on musical vibrations, colour and light, genetics and the chemistry of washday.

An article in May's *Home & Country* gave arguments for and against 'allowing the patenting of genetically engineered organisms', as a precursor to the Rio Earth Summit, and members, concerned that progress at the Summit was slow, sent a fax from the June IGM urging ratification of the biodiversity convention.

The WI has always been a leading campaigner in promoting the importance of life-long learning. Having campaigned strongly the previous summer, on the importance of funding for Adult Education, the WI continued to urge the Department for Education & Science to provide classes and non-vocational courses that did not lead to qualifications.

A five-day *Festival of Europe* course at Denman College promoted greater understanding of the European Community and the importance of partnerships.

The NFWI/RLSS project, to *Turn Bystanders into Lifesavers*, the challenge marking the Queen's 40th anniversary, won a gold medal.

Members continued to knit jumpers for destitute children in the *Jhuggi* slum areas of Delhi.

Guernsey members, and others, campaigned successfully for a free breast screening service.

Resolution: *This meeting wishes to increase awareness of endometriosis and urges the government to allocate finance to enable a higher level of research.*

Studley Lunchtime WI, *Warwickshire*

1993

Bill Clinton inaugurated as President of the US.

Northern Ireland Peace Pact signed.

• • •

The Princess Royal was the keynote speaker at the NFWI/NFU's *Caring in the Countryside* conference. This highlighted the problems of rural deprivation, the decline of the agricultural industry, the implications of rail and post office privatisation, and the loss of essential services. It also stressed the importance of working in partnership.

An initiative by two **South Yorkshire** members, inspired by visits to Romania delivering aid, resulted in a ten-year project, the aim of which was to develop a women's group in Tirgu Mures, similar to the WI. Members from 12 federations ran workshops, including dressmaking, craft, keep fit, aromatherapy, and training, in both countries, and, in 1998 the Women's Forum in Mures County was formed. With the continued help and support of WI members, its headquarters was bought in 2000.

The NFWI became a founder member of the Fair Trade foundation. A *Conserving Britain's Countryside* course was held at Denman and the WI had a high profile in the second national Adult Learners' week.

Botley WI (Hampshire) re-formed, members having discovered that, 'Like a lot of things, the WI had been taken for granted and wasn't really missed until we lost it'.

Resolution: *This meeting calls upon the Home Secretary and the Lord Chancellor to carry out a review of the Homicide Act and the criminal justice system, believing that there is an urgent need for reform of the definition of provocation to include prolonged domestic violence.*

***Clare WI**, Suffolk West*

1994

Creation of the World Wide Web.

The Church of England ordains women priests.

• • •

Members returned over 7,780 responses to the NFWI's *Caring for Rural Carers* questionnaire, sent out in 1993. The results were presented to the House of Commons in January and a conference was held in the Autumn to launch the *Nine Point Plan for Action*. The NFWI worked closely with the Carers National Association (now Carers UK) to raise awareness of the problems facing rural carers.

Exploratory talks were held with City & Guilds about joint certification. This led to a pilot scheme being set up in Patchwork & Quilting in 1996/97, with funding from the Department of Education & Employment, and other courses in Calligraphy, Sugarcraft and Cooking followed.

The final of the first NFWI Bowls Tournament was held in **Leicestershire**.

Surrey organised a *Women Aware* conference with Surrey County Council and the Surrey Police Force.

Talaton WI (Devon) was instrumental in keeping its village shop open.

An **Acton & Reaseheath WI** (Cheshire) member appeared on BBC 1's *Food and Drink* programme.

A member from **Ripon Centre WI** (North Yorkshire West), writing from experience gained while serving on Europe's Consultative Assembly from 1982-90, in an article in *Home & Country*, urged members to vote in the European elections.

Resolution: *In order that the courts may deal effectively with those who produce and purvey material of a most explicit and violent content, the government should be urged to review the unworkable key legal test in the Obscene Publications Act.*

Cheshire

1995 - 2005

Campaigning locally and globally for sustainable development.

Members of the NFWI campaign at Westminster.

Post Office campaign

Poster in support of local trade

Supporting Fair Trade

'The memory of a visit to the 'little shed at the bottom of the garden where the first WI meeting took place' on Anglesey, has stayed with me ever since — such an unimportant beginning to such a wonderful Movement.'

A member

'Belonging to the WI can make you realise your full potential — both as an individual and as a member of a national campaigning group.'

A member

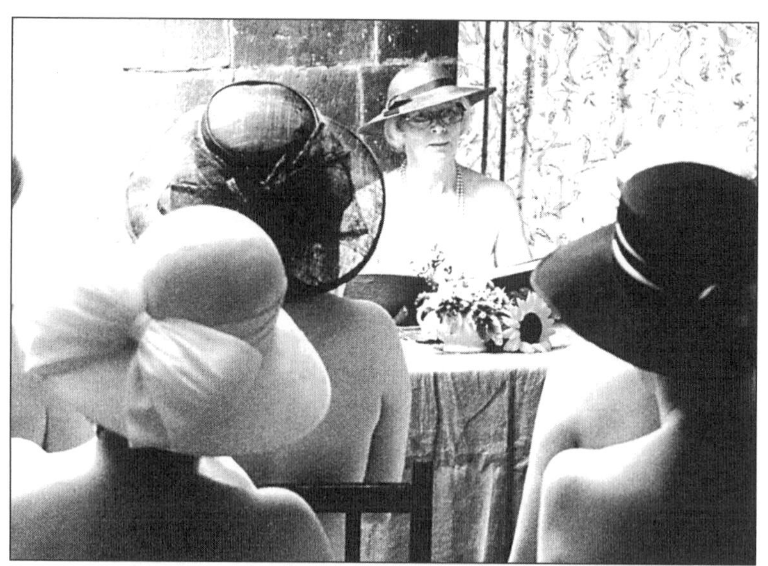

'The Calendar Girls' provided the WI with plenty of favourable publicity.

In 2000 there were 220,000 members.

1995

Fourth UN Global Conference on Women is held in Beijing.

The WWF says that the Asian tiger is facing extinction.

• • •

Denman College celebrated the 50th Anniversary of the decision to set up an adult educational college, with a *Fanfare*. Involving over 900 members, the history of Marcham Park was described in music, song and dance to over 15,000 visitors. Members of **Hampshire** and **Gloucestershire** shared the huge task of catering for thousands, providing fresh produce daily. A **Hampshire** member commented that, 'From our arrival in a borrowed pick-up truck looking like Steptoe's cart, to the daily peeling of five dozen eggs, often undertaken in the small broom cupboard (to keep cool!), no one complained'.

Lyndsay Hacket-Pain, former national vice-chairman, and World President of ACWW, reported from the Beijing Conference on Women that, 'The bulk of women's work is not recognised in statistics and their status in society does not reflect their contribution'.

Responding to the government's *Health of the Nation* initiative, the NFWI launched its successful *Best Foot Forward* campaign, for which it won a Health Alliance Award in April 1996. Its many supporters included a **Clwyd Denbigh** member who hiked 181 miles along Offa's Dyke.

Wiltshire members, armed with tape measures, surveyed local authority maintained loos in support of a resolution to enlarge ladies' lavatories. This led to a change in building regulations.

Resolution: *This meeting urges the government to ensure that food is labelled with all the contents stated, to avoid the hazards of a fatal allergic reaction from hidden ingredients.*

Quintrell Downs WI*, Cornwall*

1996

UN General Assembly endorses comprehensive Test Ban Treaty.

Massacre in school at Dunblane in Scotland.

• • •

The seriousness with which the scientific world was now taking the WI's commitment to Science was illustrated by the British Association for the Advancement of Science's invitation to exhibit at its Annual Festival of Science. *Burst the Bubble, Explode the Myth* was the appropriate theme of the NFWI's exhibit.

Following the 1995 Pensions' Bill, which equalised state pension ages, the NFWI produced a Survey Report on *Women & Pensions*. This raised awareness of the necessity of pension provision for retirement, especially in younger women. Having previously asked the government, in 1961, to recognise the unpaid work that women and carers did, the NFWI again asked for credits to be contributed towards their pensions.

Work continued on *Local Agenda 21* and, with funding from the Countryside Commission, a course was held at Denman to raise awareness of the increasing challenges threatening the quality of life of our communities and to suggest ways in which members could take action.

A **Sheepscombe WI** (Gloucestershire) member became the first British woman to compete in the *Marathon des Sables*. Running a distance of 144 miles across the desert, she had to carry all food and equipment (except a tent) and had an allowance of nine litres of water per day to cover all her needs!

Resolution: *This meeting views with grave concern the increasing lack of NHS dentists and urges the government to ensure that NHS dental treatment is available, and readily accessible, to all.*

***Kings Sutton WI**, Northamptonshire*

1997

Death of Diana, Princess of Wales.

Dolly the sheep becomes the first cloned adult animal.

• • •

The NFWI joined Greenpeace, the Green Alliance and others in expressing its concern to the government about the benefits of biotechnology, 'wary, after the BSE crisis, about reassurances from government and the food industry'.

The *Get Cooking* project, aimed at showing people how to eat healthily and cheaply, took off in the Rhondda Valley in Wales and the NFWI *Travelling Tutors*' scheme received Lottery funding, enabling it to offer greater learning opportunities to members and non-members in rural communities. The NFWI launched its Mathematics network.

Hampshire held a video conference, to celebrate the centenary of the WI in Canada, linking the national chairmen of Canada, South Africa, Australia and New Zealand with the NFWI chairman, who shared a message of support from the Queen.

A member from **Chavey Down WI** (Berkshire) became the first person to be awarded the joint NFWI/City & Guilds Patchwork & Quilting certificate. She completed a two-year course in 18 months and went on to demonstrate at Denman College.

A children's football tournament, postponed from a Family Fun Day in **Ceredigion**, led to an annual Primary Schools' Football Tournament which now involves nearly 300 children, parents, coaches and friends, with WI members (now known as the Hot Dog Football Ladies!) providing refreshments, which include hot dogs and Welsh cakes.

Resolution: *This meeting urges all WI members to support 'Agenda 21' and to work to further its social, economic and environmental aims.*

Northamptonshire

1998

UN signs treaty to set up the International Criminal Court at The Hague.

£2 coin comes into circulation.

• • •

The NFWI project, *Pathway to the 21st Century – Celebrating our Communities*, was launched, and members were urged to undertake local projects that would preserve and improve the quality of life for future generations.

Denman College's Golden Jubilee was celebrated in a variety of ways, including a *Recipe for Life* conference, sponsored by the Medical Research Council and the Biotechnology and Biological Sciences Research Council. Topics for discussion included: Food Components – good or bad for you; Chemicals/Natural Preservatives and Food Safety; and Genetics & Diet.

Suffolk East and **Suffolk West** launched their WI/SC Degree, in partnership with Suffolk College, and the following year 28 students enrolled.

Nottinghamshire began fund-raising in support of the Soroptomist's International scheme, to build a new breast care centre for local women. The final donation was £50,000.

North Yorkshire East campaigned vigorously against a 50-mile chain of massive pylons marching across beautiful countryside, and raised their objections with representatives from the National Grid.

Hawarden WI (Clwyd Flint) began work on a huge Millennium collage, now on display at St Deiniol's library as part of its Gladstone exhibition. Two books, *Work in Progress* and *Historic Hawarden*, were written to describe the project.

Resolution: *This meeting urges the government to ensure that full support is available to assist school-aged children who are carers in order that their welfare and education are protected.*

***Broughton Pastures WI**, Buckinghamshire*

1999

Devolution for Scotland and Wales.

Y2K fails to materialise.

• • •

Problems facing rural communities, the decline in the agricultural industry and the challenges of sustainable development continued to be emphasised this year. Responses to the NFWI's *The Changing Village* survey report highlighted four significant changes within villages – more housing, closure of shops and post offices, an increase in traffic and declining levels of public transport.

The Princess Royal was the keynote speaker at the NFWI/NFU *Women in Farming* conference.

Sport and leisure activities continued to be popular and the NFWI held an Open Golf Croquet tournament and an Open Crown Green Bowls tournament. The final of the NFWI Choir Festival was held in London.

A dripping tap, symbolising waste, emphasised the message of **Buckinghamshire**'s *Really Useful Day*, sponsored by Wycombe District Council, which taught that everyone must reduce, re-use and re-cycle.

A wall hanging was unveiled, created by **Teesside** members and local art students, with an *Arts 4 All* grant.

Members of **Dale WI** (Pembrokeshire) were inundated with photographs, maps, plans, newspaper cuttings and personal recollections when they started their illustrated village book project. The 96-page history was published the following year and the research material will be used for future talks.

Members of **Rylestone WI** (North Yorkshire West) launched the *Alternative WI Calendar*, which provided a great deal of unlooked-for and favourable publicity for the organisation.

Resolution: *The NFWI urges the government to introduce a minimum five-year moratorium on the commercial growing and import of genetically engineered foods.*

***Ickenham Village Afternoon WI**, Middlesex*

2000

First draft of human genome map.

UK fuel protest rattles the government.

• • •

A two-day event at Wembley Arena included the TGM, the *Woman 2000* exhibition and the Science conference on climate change and global warming, *Our Planet Earth – Know it to Manage it*, hosted with the Natural History Museum. The Prime Minister's visit to the TGM attracted considerable media attention and led to many people 'discovering' the WI. The NFWI website was launched.

A Craft Spectacular, celebrating 85 years of craft, held at Tatton Park in Cheshire, illustrated the WI's 'long-standing commitment to traditional crafts, and their importance and value in the life of the local community and the people who live there'.

Members campaigned locally to support British agriculture, with a *Buy British – Buy Local* fortnight, and an online postcard campaign, *Farming is Everyone's Business*. The NFWI, with sub-postmasters and sub-postmistresses, lobbied MPs to keep post offices open, and handed in a petition to Downing Street.

To mark the Millennium, **Hampshire** members, including at least one unsuspecting husband who stoically dyed his hair 'permanently' black, took part in *Armada to the Moon*, a story of social, sexual and technological change between the two Elizabethan ages.

North Yorkshire East members, over two weeks, handed on craft skills to 3,385 primary school children.

West Sussex instigated a Carer's Bursary (including care fees for the dependant) for a member, who was a carer, to go to Denman College.

Resolution: *We urge the government greatly to improve the treatment and therapies available to stroke sufferers, to achieve a far higher national standard of care.*

***Westonzoyland WI**, Somerset*

2001

World Trade Centre in New York is destroyed.

Foot & Mouth outbreak in the UK.

• • •

Not surprisingly, following the Foot & Mouth outbreak, farming and food issues continued to predominate this year. Key recommendations from the NFWI to the government's Policy Commission on the future of food and farming included, 'joined up policies on agriculture, sustainable development and climate change', 'support for family farms' and 'funding for local and regional food projects'.

Responses to a *Volunteers' Hours* survey, from 1,000 WIs, showed that their members devoted 3,477,312 hours to voluntary work every year. **Breadsall WI** (Derbyshire) was awarded a *Certificate of Achievement* by *Unigate Age Resource* for its voluntary activities.

An impressive range of speakers, headed by Professor Graham Macgregor, underlined the links between diet and health at a *Picture of Health* conference at Denman College, sponsored by *LoSalt*.

The NFWI joined the Jubilee Debt campaign and the Trade Justice movement, and supported the Fair Trade foundation over the challenges facing fair trade in the banana market.

The joint **Suffolk West**'s and **Suffolk East**'s *Suffolk Landscape Survey Millennium Project*, involving over a thousand members, won a Royal Town Planning Institute Award.

St Breward/St Tudy WI (Cornwall) won Best Production and Best Written Play in the NFWI's Drama Festival for its play, *Treseder's Seeds*.

Resolution: *This meeting calls upon the government to order a thorough and fully independent investigation into the causes, consequences and handling of the recent Foot & Mouth disease outbreak, and to take the necessary action at all levels to ensure a sustainable future for farming and our rural communities.*

NFWI Board of Trustees

2002

The Queen's Golden Jubilee.

Euro becomes official currency of 12 European countries.

• • •

'Put people and our planet before profit and politics.' This message from a WI member, in response to the NFWI, *What Women Want* postcard campaign, summed up the concerns expressed by members, ahead of the Earth Summit in Johannesburg.

The NFWI was invited to sit on the Government's Rural Affairs Forum for England, supported the *Your Countryside, You're Welcome* campaign, and submitted evidence to the European Parliament's enquiry into the Foot & Mouth outbreak.

Constitutional changes were decisively approved at the IGM and the three-year *Community Challenge* project was launched.

In order 'to raise awareness of energy conservation and related environmental issues', **Devon** sent a self-analysing questionnaire, containing advice for improving energy efficiency and applying for grants, to nearly 300 WIs. Follow-up work was supported by Devon County Council and the Energy Efficiency Advice Centre.

Somerset attracted up to £60,000 in funding from the Learning and Skills council to enable specialist tutors to run a variety of countywide classes.

Information gathered from the analysis of the **Sir Gar - Carmarthenshire**'s *Flora and Fauna* project, undertaken by all the members, was disseminated to local and national conservation bodies for use in future research on local environmental changes.

Resolution: *This meeting urges the government to support existing small abattoirs and promote the re-establishment of local abattoirs in order to minimise stress to animals, reduce the risk and spread of disease, and encourage the availability of locally produced meat.*

***Longtown & District WI**, Herefordshire*

2003

Iraq war declared.

Congestion charge for vehicles introduced in London.

• • •

The NFWI, with the Co-operative Bank, supported the launch of the WWF's campaign, *Chemicals & Health*, and responded to the European Commission's consultation on its proposal for a new EU regulation for chemicals.

'WI members can play a key part in shaping policies that affect our lives', was the message at the *Understanding Europe and Influencing Policy* conference at Denman College. And the relationship between health and the environment was stressed at another conference, jointly funded by The Waterways Trust and the RSPB.

The *Calendar Girls* film provided good publicity for the organisation, and WI members enjoyed the première and special showings of the film.

Flora margarine sponsored the AGM and five members completed London's *Flora* marathon.

Cumbria-Westmorland won an *Interpret Britain* award for its *Millennium Costumes'* project, for which members had made exquisite replica garments, from Tudor times to the Swinging Sixties, for hiring out to local schools.

Four **Suffolk East** members competed in University Challenge, winning through to the quarter-finals.

A WI wildflower meadow was unveiled on the **Isle of Wight**.

The Princess Royal opened **Cornwall**'s new environmentally-friendly headquarters.

Bournville WI (West Midlands) alerted its federation to the EU proposal to abolish the British hallmark.

Resolution: *This meeting views with concern the increase in obesity and diet-related health problems in children ... and urges the government to regulate the promotion to children of foods that contribute to an unhealthy diet and to ensure increased opportunities for exercise and practical food education in schools.*

East Witton WI*, North Yorkshire West*

2004

Tsunami starts in Indian Ocean.

Flash floods devastate Boscastle, Cornwall.

• • •

Continuing its campaign, with the WWF, to raise awareness about the potential dangers of chemicals to humans, wildlife and the environment, the NFWI held a conference in London and petitioned Downing Street. Members joined forces with English Heritage to *Save our Streets* in a campaign, 'to restore the dignity and distinctive local character of England's historic urban and rural thoroughfares'.

The NFWI's archives, deposited the previous year at The Women's Library in London, were opened to public access and the National Needlework Archive project, to record the needlework textiles of the WI, was launched. The results of the NFWI's first membership survey were published.

Red kites and woodpeckers were included in the winning entry of the second NFWI/*Makower* quilt competition, won by a **Buckinghamshire** member, and **Jersey** provided funding for bat boxes.

Nine **Suffolk** members, seven with first class degrees, graduated from Suffolk College.

Bedfordshire invited speakers from the Irish Countrywomen's Association to an international evening, forging friendships for the future.

An **Oxfordshire** member cycled 312 miles in six days, journeying off tourist routes from Agra to Jaipur, in aid of CLIC.

A **Clee St. Margaret WI** (Shropshire) member took the scenic route to the AGM on her own narrow boat.

Resolution: *In view of the constantly increasing trafficking of human beings, particularly women and children, for sexual exploitation and forced labour, this meeting urges the government to put into place legislation to combat trafficking and support victims.*

West Yorkshire

2005

The 90th birthday year of the WI is being celebrated throughout England and Wales with special events, exhibitions, tree planting and parties. As part of the celebrations, the NFWI joined with Tatton Park in Cheshire to exhibit a garden, *Back to our Roots - Growing for the Future*, at the northern RHS Show in Tatton Park in July, and we were all delighted when it was awarded a gold medal. Its design incorporates a replica of the original meeting place of our first WI in Llanfairpwll.

Interviewing the leaders of the three main parties, in order to encourage members to vote in the election, *Home & Country* informed them that the WI's priorities for the new government are: children's health, climate change and the alleviation of global poverty. Also in the magazine, a young politician described the WI as having 'a large part to play in the social health of the country. Their importance must never be undervalued. Communities like the WI are what makes Society'.

Ceredigion visited members of the National Women's Council of Ireland to discuss social issues, including retirement, rural problems and pension credits, share each others cultures and do some sight-seeing. A reciprocal visit is to be arranged and, looking to the future, links with a Polish and a Czech group are planned.

Cheshire formed the first *WI in the Workplace*, **Cheshire Fire WI** in the fire station's headquarters in Winsford. **Whitley WI** (Cheshire) – of which currently I am the proud president – enjoyed the spectacular **Northern Federations**' *Extraordinary Women* exhibition in the grounds of Ripley Castle and (in true WI fashion) had a meal on the way home!

Resolution: *This meeting calls on WI members to take further action to reduce waste and conserve resources in their own homes and communities: to lobby manufacturers, retailers and decision makers to reduce waste in the production, packaging and transportation of public and consumer goods.*

NFWI Board of Trustees

COMMUNITY CHALLENGES

The three-year *Community Challenge* project, supported by *LoSalt*, comes to an end in this 90th birthday year of the WI in England, Wales and the Islands, and it is important that we see these *Community Challenges* not as the end of a project but as part of the continuing work that WI members have always contributed to their local communities. These projects, undertaken over the past three years, are part of an on-going process and illustrate the core purpose of the organisation.

In the Past ...

Writing in 1912 about the Women's Institutes, founded in Canada in 1897 and later in the United States, Belgium, France and Ireland, a historian described them as, 'an active force in all matters appertaining to household and domestic science, to woman's work on the farm and to the social conditions of the community in which they operate'. He saw the WI meeting place as an arena in which women were gaining the skills, knowledge and confidence that would enable them to play an important and valued role in their local communities.

Looking back over 90 years of the WI in Britain, it seems strange that it took so long for women in this country to appreciate what those in other countries had discovered – that they had an important and socially responsible role to play in society. But once launched in 1915, progress was rapid and productive and, from the start, our leaders were determined that the WI should have a strong purpose, and that it should educate and encourage its members to improve the quality of life of their communities in whatever practical way was possible.

Whether it was by helping the national food supply of the country with food production and animal husbandry, by supporting a local village industry through craft work, by cooking for a WI Market, by raising funds for a village hall, by lobbying for better local services and facilities or by campaigning on social, environmental or economic issues, WI members in England and Wales have made a difference locally and nationally for 90 years.

Over the past years the NFWI and the federations have launched many local, national and international projects, and a look through old issues of *Home & Country* illustrates the vast range of activities undertaken by WI members in their local communities, working in partnership with others. However, researching amongst the archives in The Women's Library in London, which is now 'home' to our archives, one particular initiative, the *Town & Country* project, launched in 1970, seems to be outstanding and bears direct relevance to our *Community Challenge* project in its purpose and diversity.

Although the earlier project had, as its aim, the furthering of greater understanding between people living in rural and urban areas, and the latter concentrated more on rural regeneration and rural disadvantage, both projects led to greater community involvement, created ongoing partnerships and raised the profile of the organisation. Both projects also had an externally funded lead officer to advise and support the federations and individual WIs, and many of the projects were remarkably similar.

For the *Town & Country* project, which culminated in a huge exhibition at Olympia, almost 12,000 members in **East Sussex** undertook a survey of the local countryside for the County Council, so that a watching brief might be kept on its future conservation, and information could be provided for the general public. **Lancashire** members acted as 'human dredging machines' to clear a local stream, **Breconshire** members restored a 14th century well, part of a castle which had originally been the residence of the Bishop of St. David's, and money was raised in **Cumberland** to restore a 19th century watering place for horses.

A sponsored walk in **Devon** raised nearly £7,000 for the National Trust to preserve one-and-a-half miles of coast near Dartmouth, and a WI inventory of disposal depots in **Worcestershire** helped to solve the problem of getting large and difficult articles collected.

***Abbotts Ann WI** (Hampshire) gives a practical demonstration of teamwork and working with the local community.*

At Present ...

At the time of writing, over 2,000 WIs have registered nearly 16,000 *Community Challenges* and raised over £1 million for local projects. These have ranged in size and ambition but all have benefited local people and communities. As a small snapshot, to date, over 400 health projects and 1000 environmental projects have been undertaken, 1,500 village halls and 1000 hospices have been helped, and 500 'litter picks' have taken place.

Trees have been planted, hedgerows surveyed and gardens tended, neo-natal bonnets and blankets have been knitted, craft skills handed on to Girl Guides, story sacks presented to primary schools, and sustainable cotton shopping bags made and given away at a local farmers' market. Shopping has been done for the elderly and those with disabilities, and *First Responder* and *Messages in a Bottle* schemes set up whereby the elderly and vulnerable are given plastic containers in which to put details of next of kin, medication, etc. The containers are then placed in their fridge where they can be found in cases of accident and emergency.

Moulsham Lodge WI (Essex) raised money for a local mental health hospital, the Linden Centre. Having asked staff at the centre what was needed, and following a discussion with fellow WI members and friends, they decided to furnish a multi-sensory room which would be stimulating for all ages and soothing for stressed staff. The local CVS gave advice on promotion and how to attract donations. The room is now furnished with muted lights, bright cushions, soft materials in calm colours which move gently in a slight breeze, and soothing music is played in the background.

Spurred on by a reference in the local paper to the distance people had to travel to their nearest children's hospice, a member of **Stag WI** (South Yorkshire) almost single-handedly started a campaign to raise money to build a local children's hospice. Battling against indifference, hostility and apathy she eventually rallied support and, with help from local organisations and the WI, the Bluebell Wood Children's Hospice, near Rotherham, became a reality.

Almost 90 *Touch and Feel* tactile books, which help to stimulate and excite younger blind and partially-sighted children, have been made by members in **West Yorkshire.** (One WI made nine books!) Using a leaflet

***West Malling WI**, West Kent, making cards with the local Guide company.*

compiled by the Embroiderers' Guild and ClearVision (a national children's Braille library) which gives advice on what fabrics, wadding and stiffening materials are practical to fulfil health and safety requirements, members made books with which children could 'feel, stroke, pull, lift, shake, sniff, rattle and squeak their way through a story'. This project has given members 'the opportunity to use skill and imagination, the fun of working in a group and the satisfaction of giving practical help where it is genuinely needed'.

Tyne & Wear South members are sharing their craft skills with primary school children to promote and develop traditional skills.

Greens Norton WI (Northamptonshire) provided items for an initiative run by Sure Start staff. Members made fabric screens to put over the backs of chairs, which can then be used to screen off small areas in a larger room and make it more inviting for the Bookstart and Story Time sessions held for mothers, and children up to two years old. The screens have large pockets for nappies, wet wipes and books. Members also made book bags, containing reading and colouring books, crayons and information on early learning skills, to be used in the local community.

A local BBC radio station production of *Down Your Way* promoted the exhibition of historical and photographic memorabilia, displays and demonstrations which **Hullavington WI** (Wiltshire) organised in the local village hall. A huge success, the exhibition was supported by all the local village clubs, schools and churches. The community spirit and feeling of well-being engendered by this event will be much needed in the months to come as, sadly, the village hall was recently consumed by fire.

Seaford Martello WI (East Sussex) helped its local museum to clean and restore exhibits that were suffering from water damage and damp. The wet and dirty work included cleaning old radios, sewing machines, cash registers and telephones. During the cleaning and polishing, new friends were made, new interests started and members learnt more about the history of their town. Some members will continue to be involved with the museum,

With the publication of their book, the *History of* ***Child Okeford WI*** (Dorset), members have not only raised awareness of the importance of the WI but have also created a valuable record and social history of an organisation that makes a valuable contribution to its local community. Members of the local community and primary school have helped **Dalwood WI** (Devon) to design and produce wall hangings for the village hall. These feature village activities, buildings and local flora and fauna. A colourful booklet illustrating the hangings, their design and construction, has been produced and provides an attractive record for posterity.

Helping to alleviate the sense of isolation felt by older people, the members of **Moor End WI** (Cheshire) organise a monthly meeting for local residents. They serve refreshments and provide transport where needed. A similar project has been started by members of **Longlevens WI** and **Horsbere WI** (Gloucestershire), following a local community project to restore, extend and refurbish their village hall. WI members in **Hexton WI** (Hertfordshire) rallied round to raise money for an under-used church, threatened with closure. It's now used by the Play Group and Keep Fit class, and recently a Medieval Banquet was held in it.

Sulby WI (Isle of Man) has collated its archives, raised money for chairs for the church hall where they meet and made bean-bags for a reception area in the Social Services department. The archives of **Abbotts Ann WI** (Hampshire) are now safely stored with the local Records Office and available for local research purposes as part of the WI's *Community Challenge*. Members have also enhanced the new emergency exit of their village hall and preserved their WI banner, made in the 1920s, with help from a local tapestry conservator.

Fund-raising for an indoor sensory garden for a local school for children with special needs by **Beddgelert WI** and **Brynrefail WI** (Gwynedd Caernarfon) included one member's epic Alpine bike ride, which covered 440 miles and climbed 52,000 feet! Other less taxing events were serving refreshments to those taking part in the Snowdon fell race in Llanberis, bingo sessions, car boot sales and a hog roast.

Litter collection, minimising waste and recycling have always been issues of concern to members and **Richmond WI** (North Yorkshire West) organised a charity recycling project and collected used postage stamps,

*Murals for the village hall produced by **Dalwood WI** (Devon) and the local community.*

old printer cartridges, mobile phones, foreign coins and spectacles. **Colden Common Evening WI** (Hampshire) designed a promotion poster, circulated all local organisations and clubs, and galvanised the local community into a giant litter pick. Local school children were invited by **Moreton WI** (Devon) to enter a poster in a competition to raise awareness about dog fouling. The prize-winning poster was circulated and the local district council delivered 'pooper scoopers' to a local shop for free distribution.

Lydford & District (Somerset) supported a local charitable association by giving individual tuition in computing to people who were housebound through disability, age or caring constraints. This has enabled them to keep in touch with friends by e-mail and to use the Internet for shopping. Members of **Kingsbridge WI** (Devon), helped by local businesses, have provided people with learning difficulties with goods they might 'wish' for but couldn't afford. These have included sofas, bedding, china, electrical goods (all tested first for safety) and carpets and, although not necessarily new, all items are in good working order.

Federation challenges have included **Norfolk**'s *Milestone Project*, which has involved members working with the Milestone Society, recording local milestones and the places from which they have now disappeared. **Lancashire**, working with Lancashire County Council, is compiling a catalogue of favourite walks around the county. Once each walk has been identified, WIs are invited to research, record and describe its distinctive historical and environmental features.

Celebrating 60 years of liberation from the German occupation, the members of **St Saviour WI** (Jersey) organised a *Liberation Tea Party* as part of the local community's *Party in the Park.*

Lobbying for better hygiene in hospitals, was the *Community Challenge* of **Cranham Engayne WI** (Essex). Members wrote to their MPs, the Department of Health and the Health Authority, proposed a resolution (sadly not short-listed) and encouraged fellow members to take up the cudgels! They also wrote to their MPs and local councillors asking for 'local schools for local children' and successfully changed the council's policy.

Sustainable bags made by ***Eyton & Wellington WI*** *in Shropshire.*

Asking the question, 'Would you give your child a glass of sea-water for breakfast?' **Devon** members campaigned for less salt to be included in processed foods. They wrote to local newspapers raising awareness of the high concentration of salt in some foods, including some breakfast cereals, and urged people to study the labels on food.

In the Future ...

Some of the projects described above will already have been completed, others will be on-going, and certain smaller projects will lead on to larger and more ambitious ones. Others have yet to be started and **East Yorkshire** is planning a federation-wide challenge similar to **West Yorkshire**'s tactile books project.

The history of the WI shows a continuous thread of community action and involvement, and it is this local participation at grass roots level that has made the WI the respected and valued organisation that it is now, and has always been, thanks to the solid foundation laid down by our earliest members. I hope that reading about these projects will spur your WI or federation on to future action.

Getting the future generation involved.

Our founder members set us a great example of public service and showed how this not only enriched their lives but also improved the quality of life of their local communities. It is important for our own personal well-being, and the health of the nation, that we continue to follow this tradition of volunteering, of service to the community, whether urban or rural, and that we continue to campaign on matters that concern us. Our voice counts and our actions are important — collectively we can make a real difference.

The First Responder scheme set up by ***Kentmere WI*** *(Cumbria - Westmorland).*

NATIONAL CHAIRMEN

'The courage to dive in at the deep end is a quality a good national chairman cannot do without!'

Pat Jacob

Lady Denman DBE 1917-46

'We must all take the responsibility of ensuring that our non-party and non-sectarian rules are kept. This is no easy task and will only be successfully accomplished if each subject is considered on its merits and the question approached from a detached point of view. If we shirk this difficult task, and discourage WIs from discussing anything that might lead to difficulties, I believe that we shall limit ourselves to trivialities and so do irreparable harm to our movement.'

Countess Albermarle DBE 1946-51

'We always said that you cannot have economic development in the countryside without parallel social development, and we use the WI as one of our instruments of social development in the villages.'

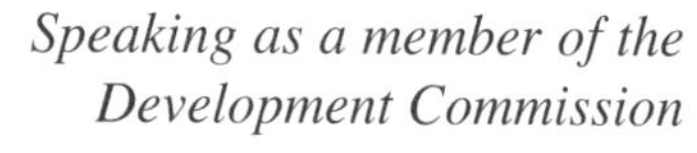

Speaking as a member of the Development Commission

Lady Brunner OBE, JP 1951-56

'I can't think how you would live in a village if you didn't belong to the WI. It would be like eating bread and milk instead of a good balanced meal.'

Lady Dyer JP 1956-61

'Discussions at the Consultative Council are like a stone thrown into a pool, with the ripples widening out until they reach the Institutes themselves.'

Lady Dyer

Mrs Gabrielle Pike CBE, JP 1961-66

'The thing about the WI is that it has always been one step ahead. The first people to bully the government about getting women policemen, the first people to bully the government to say that we must have telephone kiosks in villages. And gradually these things collected and we began to get a reputation for being the sound-box of what women wanted.'

The Marchioness of Anglesey DBE 1966-69

'When we selected resolutions it was imperative that they should be resolutions that we could do something about. Time and again we encouraged people to put forward resolutions about which, as members of a particular Institute, or as women, we could actually do something. Consumer pressure, if you like.'

Miss Sylvia Gray CBE 1969-74

'I do beg of you to live more dangerously, not recklessly, but to accept the challenge and tackle it.'

Mrs Pat Jacob Alderman JP 1974-77

'If our daughters don't join, why not? Are we old-fashioned? Are your neighbours members? How do we show that we do care about improving the quality of life for people everywhere?'

Mrs Patricia Batty Shaw CBE, JP 1977-81

'If, as we say, our broad purpose is to "give countrywomen the opportunity of working together to improve the quality of life in rural areas" then surely it must be a priority for all of us to try to do just that. Let us not allow muggers and vandals to bully the WI. Instead, the WI can take a lead in helping combat anti-social behaviour through action in the community.'

... and his Mum was a WI member!

Mrs Anne Harris CBE 1981-85

'The scope of WI activities, and the variety of ways in which we spend our time, never ceases to delight me. Many women now have jobs and young families — in some cases, both! And yet time is still found for the WI. They are attracted by the diversity and yet there is always a core of familiarity — and that's the warm feeling of friendship.'

Mrs Agnes Salter 1985-88

'We shall be making members aware of the changing face of the countryside because of changing agricultural policy and the resulting effects on rural communities. In order that they are maintained in an economically sound state, it is vital that we should be involved, as we have been so often in the past.'

Mrs Jean Varnam OBE, JP 1988-91

'Whilst always appreciating that, with such a diverse membership we all have differing views, we must also recognise that sometimes our views are in the minority and we have to accept graciously the decisions of the majority. During the next year, let's all make a special effort to exercise tolerance and accept that decisions taken on national issues do reflect the majority views — even though they may not always match with ones you hold, nor, indeed, those the executive members themselves may hold.'

Mrs Susan Stockley OBE 1991-94

'The search will soon be on for nominations for your committee. You may already have been elected. What have you taken on? A boring chore or a lively adventure? The choice is yours. Your enthusiasm and energy will bring their own rewards. The committee is at the core of every WI: it is the eye-opener, the first stepping-stone, the window which opens on to the field of opportunity. Choose your own metaphor, but remember that it is your positive attitude and your desire for wider interests in life that will determine whether or not you rise to the challenge.'

Left to right:
Anne Harris,
Patricia Batty Shaw,
Elizabeth Southey,
Lady Brunner,
Jean Varnam,
Sue Stockley.

Mrs Elizabeth Southey 1994-96

'During the year we have witnessed great achievements in each of the four corner-stones of the WI's extensive work: friendship and caring, action in the community, campaigning and influencing, and training and learning. This not only has a direct benefit to members but also, through continued commitment, it is possible for members to experience greater pleasure from seeing the impact of the WI's work in society as a whole.'

Mrs Eileen Meadmore 1996-99

'Whether you are talking to the milkman or the dentist, a friend at work or a stranger at a coffee morning, be proud of what we do and, at every opportunity, make sure you stand up for the WI — unless, of course, you happen to be driving a car at the time!'

Mrs Helen Carey OBE, DL 1999-2003

'Reading the script for the *Calendar Girls'* film recently, I was struck by a word used by one of the characters to describe what the WI gives us. Enlightenment. What a splendid word. It suggests doors opening, new discoveries, new horizons, new ideas, new skills, new ventures and sunshine. It is a happy word.'

Mrs Barbara Gill 2003-

'There is still a need to continue to fight for rural services, communities and issues that affect the lives of us all. We cannot do that unless we have a mandate on a particular issue, but once we have, through our non-party political campaigning, we can continue to use our weight and influence to try and impact change for the better.'

DENMAN COLLEGE

‘One can widen one’s horizons and let light into one’s mind.’

Sir Richard Livingstone

The idea of a WI residential college first took root in the minds of members in September 1943, during a four-day conference for WI members, on *Education and Social Security in Post-War Britain*.

The seeds of such a college had been germinating in the mind of NFWI executive member, Adeline Vernon, for some time. She believed that academic and practical education should be available to all countrywomen and she prompted the conference’s keynote speaker, Sir Richard Livingstone, president of Corpus Christi College, Oxford, and an authority on Adult Education, to put forward the suggestion that the WI should found a ‘People’s College’.

His proposition was warmly applauded by members at the conference, but in the wider membership not everyone supported the idea. Arguments both for and against such a college were widely discussed by the national executive and the federations over the next 18 months and an article was written in *Home & Country* to help clarify the debate.

Eventually the enthusiasts won over the cautious and the Consultative Council of January 1946 voted to put the resolution that, ‘This meeting welcomes the suggestion of a Women’s Institute College,’ onto the short list of resolutions for the forthcoming AGM.

Supporting the resolution, which was passed at the AGM in June 1946, NFWI executive committee member, Mrs Neville Smith, said that a WI member could 'study and discuss the questions of the day ... receive instruction and practice in the skills of the home' and that the college would 'equip her with confidence and knowledge to take a responsible position in the community'.

The next hurdle was to find a suitable house and the money to finance it. No easy task! No appropriate building could be found and the government was unwilling to provide a grant. It was not until 1947 that real progress could be seen. By then, Marcham Park had been found and an offer made. Members had raised £41,000 towards its purchase, future building requirements, furnishing and equipment, and the Carnegie Trust had promised £20,000.

The vision became a reality when Sir Richard Livingstone opened Denman College, named after our first national chairman, on 24th September 1948. The first course took place that evening and the college has been open almost continuously ever since, closing occasionally at weekends, and for cleaning and maintenance work. In past years, husbands, partners and non-members were regularly invited onto a few of the courses, but today the college is open to everyone, member and non-member alike, at all times. Outside organisations can also hire its facilities for day or residential meetings, and conferences.

So much has happened over the past 50 years to change the lives and roles of women, that the idea of a WI residential college may perhaps seem out-of-date but I believe it still has great relevance in the 21st century. It provides

Sir Richard Livingstone, Lady Brunner and Lady Denman at the opening ceremony.

The Lime Walk

an oasis of calm in a frenetic world and fulfils Lady Brunner's dream of somewhere where there is 'an inspiration and vision of wider horizons, so that life and the living of it becomes more important and more worthwhile'.

In 2005 it is expected that around 5,220 students will take almost 500 different courses and of these, 350 will be non-members.

A member, summing up the unique and priceless value of a visit to Denman in the 1960s, said, 'Only those who have been, and those that will follow after, will know the privilege I have had in going to Denman College. Believe me it has been one of the greatest joys of my life, and I mean just that.'

THE WI IN WALES

Following the formation of the first WI in **Llanfairpwll**, the organisation grew rapidly in Wales. In 1923 a Welsh speaking member was co-opted onto the NFWI, to ensure that the particular requirements of Wales were taken into account, the first Welsh Counties' Conference was organised and an honorary secretary appointed. From 1949, following the formation of a Welsh Counties Committee, its chairman became the Welsh speaking co-opted NFWI executive member. The NFWI-Wales Office was opened in Cardiff in 1980, supported by a grant of £5,605 from the Welsh Office.

The Terms of Reference of the Welsh Counties' Committee were extended in 1967 to include, 'to discuss WI matters pertaining to Wales' and in 1978, 'to consider the environment and other public issues relating specifically to Wales, especially those dealt with through the government's Welsh Office in Cardiff, and to advise the Executive accordingly.'

Health issues have featured continuously on the NFWI-Wales agenda and in 1980 it was the first voluntary organisation to become involved in the *Heart Beat Wales* programme. Other health projects have included *Lose Weight Wales* in 1991 and *Walking the Way to Health* in 2004. *Simply Good Food* was published in 1993 and in 1998 the *Get Cooking* project was launched in the Rhondda, with 23 five-week courses being delivered to 172 students.

Always keenly supportive of the Welsh language, NFWI-Wales published *Welsh for Women*, following a Welsh Learners' Course at Denman College in 1979, and started to develop its bilingual policy in 1984. In 1994-95 it was the first organisation to be included in a *Menter Iaith* (*Language Venture*) pilot project, funded by the Welsh Language Board.

The Pathway Project attracted sponsorship funding of £116,000 from the Post Office, Lloyds TSB and the Countryside Council for Wales, and the booklet, *Pathways to the Future: Case Studies for Sustainability*, was launched in 2002.

Throughout its long history, NFWI-Wales has worked closely with the government's Welsh Office, the Welsh Assembly, statutory and public bodies, and other Welsh women's organisations, on social, cultural and environmental issues, and has often 'blazed a trail' for others to follow.

Federations of Wales stand at the Eisteddfod in the 1990s.

ASSOCIATED COUNTRYWOMEN OF THE WORLD

The idea of an international rural women's conference grew from a suggestion in 1927 at a meeting of the International Council of Women (ICW) in Geneva and, thanks to the combined leadership, energy and enthusiasm of three women: Lady Aberdeen, Madge Watt and Elsie Zimmerman, the first International Conference of Rural Women was held in London in 1929, attended by 46 delegates.

A further conference, held in Vienna in 1930, agreed to carry on an informal association of countrywomen, open a central headquarters in London and hold a conference in Stockholm in 1933.

At this Stockholm meeting, an association of rural women's societies was formed, named the Associated Country Women of the World (ACWW). Madge Watt was elected president, together with eight vice-presidents. The international importance of ACWW was recognised in August 1948, when it was granted consultative status at the United Nations.

ACWW's aim has always been to improve the living standards of all women and their families, through small-scale projects. Over the years these have included: water, agriculture and craft projects in Africa and

Mrs Olive Farquharson – first Englishwoman to be elected President of the ACWW in 1971.

India, practical support in the form of medicines and equipment for hospitals in Eastern Europe, and training and empowerment programmes for women.

By the 1971 Triennial in Oslo, delegate numbers had risen to 1100 and, during the next two decades, ACWW took on a wider global remit. In support of the 1980's *Decade of International Drinking Water Supply and Sanitation*, and in partnership with UNESCO, ACWW launched two projects, *Water for All* and *Women Feed the World.*

The role of ACWW has changed considerably since 1933, when members agreed, 'to promote and maintain friendly and helpful relations between the countrywomen's and homemaker's associations of all nations and to give any possible help in their development'. A four-year project in Mali in the '90s, which provided improved access to education, health-care and income-generating opportunities for women and girls, demonstrates the vision of its founder members and illustrates the continuing importance of the work of the ACWW.

WI MARKETS

The first WI Market was opened on 19th December 1919 by **Lewes WI** (Sussex), although **Criccieth WI** (Caernarfonshire) had run a small market stall in 1916.

Wartime WI market in Malton, Yorkshire

More WI markets were formed over the following years, but it wasn't until the country faced a severe economic crisis in 1931 that the government approached the NFWI to discuss setting up markets throughout the country. This meant that markets would have to be on a more professional footing and a resolution was passed at the AGM in 1932 asking that, 'Women's Institute members should do their utmost to improve the quality and quantity of the foodstuffs they raise, increasing the amounts offered for sale through Women's Institute co-operative markets or otherwise'.

WI Markets was officially launched and, with financial support from the Carnegie Trust, who insisted that the markets should be open to both members and non-members, and to men as well as women, the NFWI was able to employ Miss Vera Cox as the first markets' organiser. The markets were registered as co-operatives under the Industrial Provident & Friendly Societies' Act.

By the end of the war there were about 300 markets and, by 1972, the annual turnover had reached £1 million, rising to £10 million by 1992. Markets' conferences have been held annually and WI markets have been represented at Ideal Home Exhibitions, the Royal Show, and many County and Agricultural Shows over the years.

In May 1995, following legal advice on charity law requirements, *WI Markets* separated from the NFWI and became *WI Country Markets Ltd* and, in May 2004, they dropped the letters WI and became *Country Markets.* They co-operate closely with *Farmers' Markets* and are represented at local events and meetings of the WI county federations.

WI Markets have presented hampers to the Queen and the Queen Mother, provided damson cheese for a banquet in honour of the King of Nepal, published *A Taste of Markets* and, in response to a challenge from *The Grocer* magazine, tested cane and sugar beet for setting qualities. With persistent lobbying by WI and market members, the 'Jam Law' was changed in 1981 and WI jam continued to be sold in WI markets.

Country Markets today

WI PUBLICATIONS

Lady Denman believed that communication between the NFWI, the federations and local WIs, was one of the most important ways of ensuring that the organisation developed in a consistent way and that every member understood the purpose of the organisation they had joined and the opportunities it offered.

Writing to WI members in 1918 in *The Landswoman* — the journal of the Land Army and the Women's Institute — Lady Denman asked local Institutes to submit reports of their activities, but these became so numerous that, in 1919, the NFWI started its own independent magazine, *Home & Country*, which has been published continuously ever since.

Lady Denman saw the WIs as an important training ground for newly enfranchised women to learn how to become active citizens and, to this end, she wrote, *Procedure at Meetings*, *The Duties of WI Secretaries*, and *Planning Work and Programmes*.

Fostering the educational aims of the organisation, the NFWI published a range of instruction leaflets, including, *Basket Willow Growing* (2d), *Games for Institute Meetings* (6d), *Maternal Welfare* (½d), *Rural Housing* (6d), and *Food Values in Cooking* (6d).

During World War II, leaflets were more about pickling and preserving, or making do and mending. Leaflets also briefed members about current issues, some of which resulted from consultation with members, such as the *Women's Institute's Views on Education* (3d).

Post-war restrictions on paper limited the range of leaflets but a later production of a series of small books on *Craft* and *Cookery* were so popular that the NFWI set up its own publishing arm. WI Books, registered as a privately owned limited company in 1977, traded successfully for some years but, with cheaper books becoming more available in the shops, in the 1990s a decision was taken to cease trading.

All WI trading is now done through WI Enterprises Ltd (WIE), which makes a sizable contribution to the NFWI each year. Its activities include the WI's *Home & Country*, *Woman's World*, the *NFWI Raffle*, and a few distinctive sales lines. WIE also seeks commercial sponsorship for Denman College, the AGM and WI mailings.

SOURCES

Andrews, Maggie, *The Acceptable Face of Feminism – The Women's Institute as a Social Movement*, Lawrence and Wishart, 1997

Davies, Constance, *A Grain of Mustard Seed*, Gee & Son Ltd. (Denbigh), 1953

Deneke, Helena, *Grace Hadow*, Oxford University Press, 1946

Dudgeon, Piers, *Village Voices*, WI Books, 1989

Garner, Gwen, *Extraordinary Women, A History of the Women's Institutes*, WI Books Ltd, 1995

Goodenough, Simon, *Jam and Jerusalem*, Collins (Glasgow and London), 1977

Home & Country, the monthly magazine of the WI, published by the NFWI since 1919

Huxley, Gervase, *Lady Denman GBE 1884-1954*, Chatto and Windus (London), 1961

Jenkins, Inez, *The History of the Women's Institute Movement of England and Wales*, Oxford, 1953

Kaye, Barbara, *Live and Learn, The Story of Denman College 1948-1969*, NFWI, 1970

McCall, Cicely, *Women's Institutes*, Collins (*Britain in Pictures* series), London, 1943

Robertson Scott, J W, *The Story of the Women's Institute Movement*, The Village Press, Idbury, Kingham, Oxon, 1925

Speaking Out, A Public Affairs Handbook, NFWI, (revised version 2001)

Stamper, Anne, *Rooms Off the Corridor, Education in the WI and 50 Years of Denman College 1948-1998*, WI Books Ltd, 1998

Working With Women Worldwide, Highlights of 75 Years of ACWW (published by ACWW) 2004

ACRONYMS

AOS	Agricultural Organisation Society
AGM	Annual General Meeting
ACWW	Associated Countrywomen of the World
CF	County Federation
CFCs	Chlorofluorocarbons
CLIC	Challenging Cancer and Leukaemia in Childhood
COPUS	Committee for the Public Understanding of Science
CVS	Council for Voluntary Service
cwt	one hundredweight
FFHC	Freedom From Hunger Campaign
FMD	Foot and Mouth Disease
HM	His or Her Majesty
IGM	Intermediate General Meeting
ITA	Independent Television Authority
KBTG	Keep Britain Tidy Group
LEA	Local Education Authority
MAFF	Ministry of Agriculture, Fisheries and Food
NFU	National Union of Farmers
NFWI	National Federation of Women's Institutes
OPEC	Organisation of the Petroleum Exporting Countries
RCC	Rural Community Council
RHS	Royal Horticultural Society
RLSS	Royal Life Saving Society
RSPB	Royal Society for the Protection of Birds
TGM	Triennial General Meeting
USSR	United Soviet States of Russia
VCA	Village Clubs Association
VCO	Voluntary County Organiser
VSO	Voluntary Service Overseas
WHO	World Health Organisation
WWF	World Wildlife Fund

ACKNOWLEDGEMENTS

I would like to thank all the federations and individual members who contributed to this book. Space hasn't allowed me to include all the material that was sent in but I have read — and listened to — all the federation and WI histories, stories, tapes, letters and anecdotes, and it has provided a fascinating record of past events, activities and campaigns, and added valuable background data. Every federation has been included — even if briefly — but with county and federation boundary changes, some of the names will have altered over the years. My research has shown that certain events have different dates in different publications and, although I have tried to allocate events to the appropriate year, certain inaccuracies may have arisen, for which I apologise.

There has been a certain quirkiness over the years in the celebration of the NFWI's 'special' birthdays! The 10th birthday is dated from the year the National Federation was formed whereas, for some reason, its 21st birthday was celebrated in 1937. From its 50th Birthday onwards, all celebrations are dated from 1915, when the first WI was formed.

My thanks to Anne Stamper, the NFWI's archivist, for her help and advice, and for sending me much of her own original material and archive photograph collection. Our NFWI archives, now safely housed in The Women's Library, Old Castle Street, London E1 7NT, were an invaluable source of inspiration and I am indebted to Susan Stockley, former national chairman and Anne Ballard, former general secretary, and others, for the many hours they spent sifting through those archives in the garage at Denman College before they went to London.

I am grateful, too, to Jana Osborne, general secretary, and all the NFWI staff in London, Wales and at Denman College, to Charlotte Foster, project officer of our Community Challenge Project (sponsored by *LoSalt*) and Midge Thomas, former chairman of WI Markets.

Nearer home, my thanks to members of Whitley WI, the Cheshire Federation of Women's Institutes and all my friends and colleagues in Cheshire for their encouragement and support.

USEFUL ADDRESSES

National Federation of Women's Institutes
104 New Kings Road, London, SW6 4LY
Telephone: 020 7371 9300
Email: hq@nfwi.org.uk
Website: http://www.womens-institute.org.uk

Denman College
Marcham, Abingdon, Oxfordshire, OX13 6NW
Telephone: 01865 391991
Email: info@denman.org.uk

Denman College today

NFWI Wales Office
19 Cathedral Road, Cardiff, CF1 9HA
Telephone: 02920 221712
Email: walesoffice@nfwi-wales.org.uk

Country Markets Ltd
Dunston House, Dunston Road, Sheepbridge, Chesterfield, Derbyshire, S41 9QD
Telephone: 01246 261508
Email: info@country-markets.co.uk
Website: www.country-markets.co.uk

Associated Country Women of the World
Mary Sumner House, 24 Tufton Street, London, SW1P 3RB
Telephone: 020 7799 3875
Email: info@acww.org.uk
Website: www.acww.org.uk

EPILOGUE

Question from schoolteacher to small boy: 'Who makes the laws and governs the country nowadays?'

Answer without hesitation: 'Please, Miss, the WI!'

Quote from the early years

Question from vicar to bishop, looking at a list of names in his diary with the initials WI after them: 'I didn't know you were involved in the Women's Institute my lord?'

Answer: 'I'm not. That means Wives Impossible and I never stay for lunch!'

Quote from the middle years

Question to builders painting the village hall, as members go in to their WI meeting: 'How are you going to cope with all those ladies?'

Answer: 'We're going home!'

Quote from today

"I hear your dear wife is to give our Women's Institute a lecture."
"My dear lady, it's no use appealing to me, I can't stop her."
(Reproduced by kind permission from "Punch.")

ABOUT THE AUTHOR

I have been a member of the WI since 1964. Having recently graduated from Trinity College, Dublin, I married and went to live in Girton village, near Cambridge, and was encouraged to join the local WI. Moving back to Cheshire four years later, having lived abroad for two years, it seemed inevitable that I would pick up the threads of WI life again.

It seemed to me to encompass everything that made life worthwhile – involvement in the local community and the countryside, educational opportunities and environmental issues, music, people — the list was endless. You really can do almost anything you want with the WI and enjoy yourself at the same time. Over the years I have been a President, WI Adviser, Chairman of the Cheshire Federation and Chairman of the NFWI from 1999 to 2003, and each 'job' has brought its own interests, rewards and new group of friends.

I am most grateful to all the members of my extended family, especially my husband, sons and sisters, not only for their help with this book but also for 'living' with the WI for so many years. They have patiently listened to me enthusing (with only the occasional complaint) about the WI for many years and have appreciated that the WI isn't just a passing interest but 'a way of life'!

My husband has nobly read through every page of this book, pointed out inconsistencies and given constructive criticism, and I am grateful that our landlady in Girton, Frida Leakey, who first encouraged me to join the WI, gave *him* such a good grounding in it at an early age!

Orchards of Cheshire, the first book I edited, was published in 1995 to celebrate 75 years of the WI in Cheshire and also to remember, and encourage, fruit growing in the county. It reflects my ongoing interest in the environment, and *Bows of Burning Gold*, of course, illustrates my abiding belief in the importance of belonging to, and being involved in, the local community.